Lost
On Purpose

PATRICK TAYLOR

Photos and maps of trek available online at
http://www.texasyetibooks.com

Cover design by Kristin Bryant
Kristindesign100@gmail.com
Cover Photo by Salajean

ISBN: 1519145373
ISBN-13: 978-1519145376

***

Other books by Patrick Taylor:

"River Hippies & Mountain Men"
"Alone on Purpose"
"Humble Heroes"
"Hardhat Ballet"

CONTENTS

"It was all I ever wanted; to be a great explorer
like the ones that occupied my dreams. But, in the end
it was not what I expected. It always seemed a solo adventure.
Even in the company of good men,
it was always a solitary journey".

- Patrick Taylor

Too Deep

It was quiet in the truck as we drove up the Bitterroot Valley. Cousin Brenda was talking, but I couldn't hear her. I was deep down inside myself trying to get past all the prep work and into the moment at hand. I looked at the Continental Divide as it stretched out on our left. It was a big high bridge to another world. For me, merging with mountains was always a soulful experience and I planned on losing myself in them again. But I was bothered by my daughter's words from our meeting the week before resounding in my head and they were unexpectedly unsettling.

"It's too deep, Dad." Her eyes filled with tears. "It's too deep to go alone."

My little girl was no longer a child; Paloma was a woman. And for all of her twenty-three years, I adventured. She had seen me leave to go ice climbing in Scotland, shark diving in Burma, deep caving in Borneo, every adventure imaginable. Never before had she said "No". She had never questioned the rationale behind an adventure; my trips were like other dad's games of golf. Then this surprising response to what was a relatively tame excursion; I did not know how to respond to her emotion. I was an empty-nester with at least 20 years left in my life and planned to enjoy many more adventures. She knew I was fit and thoroughly experienced; it couldn't be the work. Could it be because it was new terrain to me? No, she didn't think like that; besides, I climbed all over the world. Why would

Idaho suddenly seem scary? I wasn't even climbing, for Christ's sake. It was a trek; the first month was a stroll. Maybe the concern existed because she was sensitive to the impact of the divorce on me (though that was many years ago) and had grown worried about my life's trending lately. Was she worried that my head wasn't right for this challenge? Was she thinking me too old? I hadn't been able to read her as I looked into her big doe eyes, but I could tell that the concern was genuine. The fear was real. All I had been able to do was reassure her.

"Do you seriously think there's anything in those big old nasty mountains that will keep me from coming back to you?" I joked, being the tough Marine she loved and the loving daddy every girl needed. With a smile, I reached out to her, took her in my arms, and held her close in silence. She trembled. It hurt me to feel her so worried.

I looked out the window as Brenda drove down the road and thought about what Paloma said the week before, about how she looked at me. To be sure, the trek would take me deep into one of the largest wilderness areas in this vast country of ours. There were many unknowns but there always were… that's why they were called adventures. And adventures were my passion.

Brenda came back into focus and looked at me curiously as she drove.

"Did you hear anything I said?" she asked.

"Not since we drove through Sula, Montana."

She smiled and shook her head, hands at ten and two on the steering wheel. She completely shared my excitement; her support was unbelievable. Four days before, I flew into Salt Lake City from Dallas in order to see my Dad before the trek. Brenda drove down from her home and trek HQ in Salmon, Idaho to pick me up and take me back; a 7-hour drive each way. Nobody drove 7 hours to pick someone up from the airport, but Brenda did it for me. Then she drove me up to the planned midway point of the trek to scout out a spot to reprovision. That was a 6 hour round-trip… a total of 20 hours and I'd only been there for four days. If everything went according to plan, there would be another 26 hours. Brenda loved the mountains and she loved being involved in the adventure. She was as enthusiastic as I was and I remain forever grateful to my cousin Brenda for her help.

"I said we're almost to Hamilton; another ten or twelve minutes. Do we turn toward the mountain in Hamilton?"

"Yes, ma'am. Left on Main, then a right and a left. Then you can kick me out of the truck and go eat."

She had the ear-to-ear smile on her face. I knew she wanted to go. With her chin up a little, she eyeballed the mountain and chattered as we went down the road. She was savvy enough to make the trip, but bad knees prevented her from participating in anything as extreme as this crossing. When we made the left turn on Main Street, I saw the 10 mile long canyon cut through the rock.

Brenda took pictures while I geared up and the dogs ran around at the trailhead. The pre-trek tension melted away and I felt calm as I put on my gaiters.

"Damn, that pack is heavy!" she said as she tugged on the straps. "Are you sure you need all of that stuff?"

She had seen me lay everything out on the table in her home and carefully check each item off the list as it was packed. And repacked. A couple of times.

"No, I'm sure there's stuff that I forgot and plenty I don't really need," I smiled.

"How much is it?"

"Right at 60 pounds."

"Good Lord! Isn't that heavy?"

"Well, there's folks that carry more. And it's not much for a man my size. It might be a little fat, but it's winter and I can correct things when we reprovision. Remember, this has got to last a month including food." I winked.

"A month," she said wistfully. "Going backcountry alone for a month... actually, it will be closer to two." She paused in thought. "Man, I sure wish that I could go with you."

"You're more than welcome, Brenda; I hope you know you can go. I'd be happy to have you along."

"No, you wouldn't. Not this time. You're crossing the Rockies alone in winter. Up through the Clearwater. Following Lewis & Clark."

She looked down at the glove she was holding for me in her hand as if the enormity of the plan just became clear for her. She looked up sincerely into my eyes and seemed to me just like she did when we were teens in California. I looked back at her and reached out for the glove.

She asked earnestly, "What's that feel like, Patrick? Right now, when you're about to do it? What's it feel like to look at something that big?"

The answer was unfiltered, straight from my heart through my mouth to my cousin.

"Scary off and on for the last hour or so while you were driving up here. Exciting now. I've planned well and I feel prepared." I paused and finished my reply with appropriate respect, "But I am keenly aware that no one can ever be fully prepared for all that Mother Nature can throw at us. I feel like I'm stepping off an edge and the leap of faith is exhilarating."

I smiled and comforted us both.

"And honestly," I continued, "like most people, I'm anxious to know if I measure up."

"Do you know how proud I am of you?"

"You might want to save that for when I make it..." I cautioned.

"You'll make it. If anyone can, it's you." She threw her arms around my neck and gave a big warm hug. "I love you, Cuz. I need some pictures of you all geared up."

She still took pictures as I headed up the trail. It was crisp and clean in early October and she filled her day with memories of my departure.

Making It Real

A trek can be defined as 'a journey or trip involving difficulty or hardship'. The aborigines attached a spiritual aspect and value to an individual's trek - an event lasting several months which they call a walk-about. Native Americans practiced a similar cultural observance with their vision quests. I participated in all kinds of treks all over the world; there is nothing like a good long walk for clearing out the mind.

Not so much in the recent past, though; for the last dozen years or so, my participation in adventure and treks had waned. I raised a son, struggled with my businesses, and struggled with life for the first time in decades. I couldn't go trekking, but my taste for adventure stayed with me through those years. Subconsciously, I knew I needed it. In the back of my mind, I remembered that trekking always satisfied something in me that nothing else could sate. I never went trekking without coming home happy to be alive. As I continued to struggle with that last chapter in my life, I wondered if something bold might give me a little spark.

I had been caught up under the Wheel of Life for a while. Like many people, I escaped by reading. I developed a passion for the history of Lewis & Clark and read every title associated with the Corps of Discovery. I daydreamed about retracing their footsteps across the

Rocky Mountains and dropping off the grid for a while. It had been so many years since I allowed a dream to become reality in my life. I researched and prepared for what I knew intuitively could be a new and daring adventure. I cobbled together maps to determine routes and spreadsheets for the gear that needed to be assembled. I enjoyed planning an adventure – preparing for something difficult. It had been a long time since I had done something difficult with my life, a long time since I truly challenged myself and I felt the rush of blood through my body and my brain.

To me, Lewis & Clark were on the same level as astronauts; the greatest explorers of their time. Within months of their return to St. Louis, groups of men retraced their path up the Missouri to the Abundant West. It was the beginning of the age of the free trapper and a period of time that I think was important to who we were as Americans. I became fascinated by the free trappers who followed on the heels of Lewis & Clark. With no experiential knowledge of the dangers that awaited them, these adventurous entrepreneurs trapped every river and creek they could follow up a hill; every waterway that might contain some beaver. The Lewis & Clark expedition opened the door to a frenzy of exploration and exploitation. And none of that growth, none of the commerce that brought people west would have been possible without the successful crossing of the Rocky Mountains by Lewis & Clark after they left the Missouri River.

Somewhere between growing tired of a life that wasn't working anymore and immersing myself in a tale of great adventure was when the whole Lewis & Clark trek began to manifest itself as a reality for me. I looked at maps of their route through the mountains, how they started in Montana and finished crossing the mountains in Idaho. I broke it down into manageable chunks. It was too hard to think about walking all the way across the Rocky Mountains, but I had done lots of 20 and 30-mile trips so I looked at the map through that lens. Smaller chunks made it seem more attainable. All of this work, of course, told my subconscious mind that the adventure was possible. And when that happened, all kinds of important things began to happen for me.

I spent time estimating how long it would take to cross the Rockies. How long would it take to cross more than 200 miles of mountains and what was a reliable pace to use as a forecasting tool? 20 miles a day? In the steep Idaho Rockies? With a 60-pound pack in the snow? Maybe 10 miles a day was more realistic; maybe eight would be better. That calculated out to be 25 travel days and I certainly had no intention of traveling every day. Traveling every other day for 8 miles made it a sixty-day trip.

And how much food would I need? This proved to be the best question asked during the planning process. A traditional rule-of-thumb was one and one-half to two pounds of food per day per hiker. Obviously, that rule-of-thumb was suspect; there was no known correlation between the weight of food and its caloric/nutritional value. If I used the traditional approach, I had to plan on carrying 45-60 pounds of food for a month (along with all my other gear). Instead, I decided to be creative and design a diet to provide the best calorie/weight ratio. I calculated answers and refined them and, in doing so, began to believe that it was possible to carry enough food to cross the mountains alone.

"I could handle three or four weeks out alone. Just a little longer than the trip to Washakie in Wyoming."

I used the fact that I had gone backcountry off-season for ten days in deep winter to rationalize the trek. I had experienced the high country in the winter; I soloed Wyoming's Washakie Wilderness outside Yellowstone during February one year. I possessed experience that I could leverage while crossing the Rockies.

"I can carry food for a month, but I'm going to need a drop or something. All I will need is a single reprovisioning of food and I can make it all the way across."

The answers weren't just Walter Mitty fantasy answers to a time-killing daydream, but serious answers arrived at by consideration of the facts. I had experienced the high country in winter. I possessed a good understanding of wilderness navigation. It may have been years since my last outrageous adventure had occurred, but I was still a mountaineer. I practiced the dialog, seriously considered my options, and - somewhere deep inside of me – my subconscious had already made the commitment to this new high country quest.

I looked for opportunities to reinforce my belief and bring the plan into life. I discussed it with friends.

"Yeah, I was reading a book about Lewis & Clark and thought it'd be cool to do the same thing."

"Same thing as what?" a friend asked as we moved down the lunch counter.

"Cross the Rockies on the Lewis & Clark trail."

It didn't matter how the friend responded or if he responded at all. I said the words for myself; not anyone else. In my mind, the adventure was becoming a reality. An increasingly important one; there was more to this trek than fun. I engaged in plenty of thrill-seeking throughout my life, but this trek was as much about self-seeking as adventure-seeking. No matter how crazy it appeared to others, I knew I needed it and had to make it happen.

People need adventure in their lives to give the tedious day-to-day struggle meaning, to create a purpose greater than going to work and paying bills. Most of the adventures in my life were planned. It was easy to forget – and it happened to me – that we must make time for adventure or run the risk of living life without it.

I sought to put my physical and emotional energy into something positive, energizing, and expansive rather than allow myself to dry up and waste away in a life of unwanted expectations. It became symbolic of breaking away from a funk that had threatened the best of me. The trek was big and difficult and appropriately dramatic, and it started off as a nothing more than a crazy idea. It was time to put adventure in my life again, no matter how crazy the adventure seemed.

The focal point of the trek was to follow in the steps of Lewis & Clark's Corps of Discovery journey across the Rocky Mountains. I would start in Montana close to the Continental Divide not far from where Lewis first looked out over the mountains. As the Lewis & Clark party moved west from Montana's Lolo Pass, their guide led them on a path parallel with and north of the Lochsa River. It took them 19 days to cross the Rockies before they reached the plains of western Idaho. When I finished the route I planned to Kooskia, Idaho, I could rightly claim to have traversed the Rockies alone.

I studied with whole-hearted dedication the route taken by the Corps of Discovery. The study opened my eyes to how much had changed since they traveled from St. Louis to the coast of Oregon. In the two hundred years that followed their exploration, the great Missouri River (which was wild and unmapped in their day) had become generally safe and somewhat boring. To a trekker like me, walking hundreds of miles across the plains of Montana and the Dakotas would hardly qualify as an adventure. A challenge perhaps but not an adventure. The most difficult section of the Lewis & Clark affair came when they had to cross the Rockies in September and that was the part that I wanted to experience. They crisscrossed up the side of a mountain until they got to the top of a ridge. From there, they surveyed the surrounding mountains and planned a route by connecting ridgelines that took them where they wanted to go. Lewis & Clark did their best to run the 'hog backs' of what is now the Clearwater National Forest. They searched the ridgelines for paths through the mountains that led to the plains and the Columbia River. We didn't know exactly where they went, but we knew how they navigated, their tendencies while trailblazing. Many landmarks of their journey across the mountains still existed and much of the trail was still used, but large sections of it had disappeared and academics argued about the path actually taken by the Corps.

"What about standing where Lewis stood?" I considered. "How cool would it be to see the Rockies the way he saw them the very first time from Lemhi Pass?"

It was said that shortly after finding the source of the great Missouri River, Lewis climbed up to Lemhi Pass. It was there he first gazed out on the magnificent Rocky Mountains. The Mandan Indians, with whom they had wintered the year before in present day North Dakota, had advised him he could cross the mountains in 'five sleeps'. How anxiety-ridden poor Lewis must have been when he finally saw the mountains for himself. Wave after wave of impassable peaks stacked up beyond the horizon; it would take more than 'five sleeps' to get across those mountains and they had not the luxury of time. He hurried to meet up with Clark and together they went in search of horses. The Corps of Discovery moved north through what was renamed the Bitterroot Valley. They found Shoshone Indians with whom they bargained for horses and crossed into the mountains by Lolo Pass.

My initial plan was to see what he saw; to know the feelings that Lewis felt looking at the mountains from Lemhi Pass. And I could do that; I could get up to Lemhi Pass, but hiking from there to Lolo seemed pretty pointless. That region was covered with ranches and the Bitterroot Valley was narrow, domestic, and full. It served no purpose to hike 90 miles up a highway to reach the crossing at Lolo Pass just for the sake of historical accuracy.

I was not much for hiking valleys, anyway; I had always been more of a ridge-running kind of guy. I liked it where the wind blew hard enough to shape the landscape and you could hear it coming for miles. I liked it where your eyes saw all the mountains around you and picked a path along the shoulders of giants. The only wind on the Bitterroot Highway would be from oncoming traffic. I decided to bypass Lemhi Pass and the Bitterroot Valley, and I looked for something a little more fun.

One of the most attractive parts of the western edge of the Bitterroot Valley was that it bordered with the Selway-Bitterroot Wilderness, the 2nd largest contiguous wilderness in the Lower 48. The Selway-Bitterroot Wilderness area boasted 1.4 million acres kept pristine by congressional act. It was a place that "man may visit but may not remain." Further research showed me that it was bordered on the south by the Frank Church – River of No Return Wilderness. The Frank boasted over 2.2 million protected acres and held the title of the largest contiguous wilderness area in the Lower 48. The two areas combined to become the largest mountainous wilderness outside Alaska. A person could literally spend years in there and never pass the same patch of ground. Trekking through the Selway-Bitterroot Wilderness sounded a lot more interesting than hiking up the Bitterroot Valley, so I it worked into my plan.

I studied maps and determined that much of the eastern end of the Lolo Trail (Lewis & Clark's trail through the Rockies) – the part in the state of Montana - had been commercialized. Until one arrived at Wendover Ridge, their trail had been tamed and rendered boring. I devised a plan that allowed me to trek through the Selway-Bitterroot Wilderness working my way northwest for a few weeks and then connect to the Lewis & Clark trail at Wendover Ridge. That seemed ideal; I could challenge myself with a month alone in one of the most remote mountain regions in the country and then reprovision to tackle the most difficult part of the greatest American adventure of all – Lewis & Clark's trip across the mountains. And by putting the two routes together, I could traverse the Rocky Mountains.

From what I saw on the maps, I could reach the edge of the wilderness area by going on a 10-mile hike up a canyon that led to Blodgett Pass on the western edge of Hamilton, Montana. Then I would cross over the pass and into the northeastern quarter of the Selway-Bitterroot Wilderness. From there, I would spend weeks casually exploring the great wilderness before I crossed over to the Lewis & Clark trail. It would be a very long trip; 6 or 8 weeks to cover close to a couple hundred miles on foot in steep mountains and snow.

I originally planned to go during the winter. It was my preference; there were no bears, no snakes, and no people in the mountains during the winter so it was clearly the best time to go. But Park Rangers and Search and Rescue folk were not big fans of people going out in the winter alone. Especially in Idaho; not when I told them where I wanted to go. They had some strong opinions on that subject.

"I wouldn't recommend you be there in the deep winter, Mr. Taylor."

"In where, ma'am? On that trail?"

"No, sir; in the Clearwater. Those mountains are so steep and so close together... it's like avalanche crossfire. You should be out of there no later than November. Be home for Thanksgiving. Those storms will start overlapping and you'll be snowbound."

"I understand, ma'am. But I have experience in extreme environments at higher elevations and I'm a pretty capable pathfinder..."

"Unfortunately, sir, your lack of winter experience in the Clearwater drainage, the Lochsa drainage, and the Selway drainage disqualify you from engaging in the activities you list. It's a free country and we can't stop you from going. But, with all due respect, you called for advice and my advice is to try it our way one year and we'll talk again later. For what it's worth, I've never heard of anyone hiking Lolo in November and there's probably a reason for that. Take what it gives you and make sure you can bail out. If you get into big weather on Lolo, use your compass and head south. Head down to where the snow turns to rain and you might get out."

I listened to her through the phone and no ego or opinion echoed in her voice. She merely stated fact. She seemed very interested in the route selection and was intrigued by my food plan but remained matter-of-fact about getting out before Thanksgiving. The storms that blew in from the Pacific were moisture-laden storms that rarely made it past the Continental Divide. They were rolled back on top of themselves to unload thick wet layers of snow on the short tree-covered mountains. It was common practice for trekkers like me to wait three days after storms for avalanche danger to settle, but new storms rolled into Idaho before the last ones had time to settle. The end result was very deep, very wet snow that became impenetrable in spots. I was glad she communicated her concern.

Similar conversations convinced me to take the advice to heart and set my start date to October for the Selway-Bitterroot section and November for the Lewis & Clark section.

My idea to relive the Lewis & Clark experience transformed into a reality. The original idea morphed into a workable plan one piece at a time. I would get used to pack weight, navigation and pace, and general energy requirements while I trekked the Selway-Bitterroot Wilderness in October. Then, fit and fine-tuned, I would retrace the Lewis & Clark trail during the first half of November. I would complete my trek just as the serious snows arrived. Given that I was starting a month later than Lewis & Clark, the weather would likely be at least as nasty for me as it was for my heroes.

The trek was more than just an extreme camping trip; it was an open-ended commitment to adventure. One adventure often opened doors to other adventures. It was to be the new chapter in my life. I imagined a romantic existence where I lived alone happily ever after wandering through the mountain wilderness like John Colter. Where all the responsibilities and expectations that I had drug around finally fell away long enough for me to remember Me. Not forever; not a divorce from my life. I called it a sabbatical, an extended Leave of Absence from all the demons that had been eating my soul.

With my trip route planned, I began to build a gear list. Gear selection for the trip was fairly straightforward. The basics for any trek were always the same: food, shelter, and water. Shelter was divided into sub-groups like tents, bivy sacs, sleeping bags, and clothing. Winter camping required more equipment, more layers of clothing, a heavier tent and sleeping bag. I had no room for luxuries. The season dictated the selection of a -20 degree sleeping bag, an ultra-light design at 3.75 pounds. The trip would subject me to extremes and that meant I needed the most reliable gear. My choice for a tent was made in Sweden where they know something about the cold. The orange tube tent was my preferred lightweight all-season tent. Of course, I would layer clothing to meet the needs of the day. I packed two pairs of base layer 'long johns' made of a poly/wool blend to keep my skin dry and would alternate them every day. I would wear a down jacket and appropriate pants, probably fleece or wool, as a 2nd layer. The 3rd shell layer would be Gore-Tex. If one is going to spend time in the backcountry – especially in the winter – that person is wise to have Gore-Tex. I might add a sweater to give some extra warmth but only one. Also, any alpinist needed a strong water-resistant, expedition-grade pack; if your pack wasn't water-resistant, everything in it got wet, whether it was storming or not. And damn good boots; to me, boots were most important. They should be strong and flexible with a good edge for cutting steps. Waterproof, of course.

I selected all these items off a spreadsheet I had assembled over my career as an alpinist and amateur adventurer. My spreadsheet had the description and weight of every item that I owned - in ounces. It was a science, really. I had to keep my pack weight under 40 pounds in the summer and no more than 60 pounds in the winter if I wanted to cover long distances. Lighter was better, but care had to be taken to ensure I had what I needed to complete a successful trek. My spreadsheet was a personal tool specific to my gear collection. When I selected the pack items I needed for a trip, the spreadsheet calculated my pack weight instantly and I could then make adjustments accordingly. I knew exactly what my load would weigh before I start packing.

I needed up-to-date maps in my GPS and packed my Personal Locator Beacon (PLB) for emergencies. The locator beacon was not a SPOT device. While similar to a PLB and handy for local communication, the SPOT sent out an emergency signal at a relatively weak 0.4 watts of transmission energy on a commercial satellite network sharing bandwidth. My PLB used a dedicated military satellite network managed through NOAA. My device transmitted at 5.0 watts, 12.5 times the power of SPOT. The PLB didn't offer many messaging features, but it guaranteed a priority connection to a Search and Rescue team. It was superior technology and part of my safety plan; "be self-reliant, leave plans with pros, and have a PLB." When activated, my emergency device would send a NOAA-validated distress call out to the network of SAR units in the geographic location identified in the distress signal. The PLB transmitted two frequencies; one to bring the rescuers within 100 yards and a second signal to hone in on a strobe light. I even purchased LifeFlight insurance to cover the cost of helicopter transport in an emergency.

I couldn't help thinking that my greatest opportunity for innovation would be my food selection. I knew one of the great challenges in planning the trip revolved around packing enough food for that period of time while maintaining a manageable pack weight. I would have to get creative in designing a menu because food for long trips weighed a lot and minimizing weight was top-of-mind with trekkers. For many people on the trail, meals were a big part of the trip. A lot of effort and a lot of different food items could be used to design a menu for a trip. And there were few things as satisfying after a long day of hiking as a tasty hot meal by the fire. While I had no aversion to fine foods, I felt a Spartan-like approach made more sense for my project. I decided to take thinking about food out of daily activities. I could simplify things greatly if I ate the same things every day. I could pack in bulk; 30 bags of oatmeal dumped into a single Ziploc. Two large jars of protein powder dumped into gallon Ziploc. The same for trail mix and peanut butter. I minimized trash that I would have to pack out and kept things simple and light. In my mind, the final diet should have the appropriate proportions of protein, fat, and carbohydrates (with an emphasis on protein) while maximizing the calorie/weight ratio. The end result of this somewhat eccentric approach to daily meal planning was as follows:

- ½ cup oatmeal
- 2 tablespoons peanut butter
- Jerky and trail mix
- 1 cup protein powder drink (at end of day's hike)
- 3 ounces tuna fish (in pouch)

Total calories per day = 1020 calories

Total weight per day = 9 ounces (compared to the 1 ½ - 2 pounds an average hiker packed)

At first, I thought I sacrificed too much. Most people burned more than twice that amount in an average day. But a pound of fat was equal to 3500 calories, so if I burned 500 more calories than I consumed each day 7 days a week, I'd lose one pound of fat in a week. If my body burned 2000 calories a day and I only consumed 1000 calories of fuel, I'd lose 2 pounds that week. At that rate, I would lose 12 pounds during a 6-week trek and that wouldn't hurt me at all. Of course, I would burn more than that on the more strenuous parts of my journey, but I planned to supplement my menu using a fishing rod and slingshot. In the final analysis, I 'guesstimated' that I would lose a little more than 20 pounds during the trek and that was acceptable to me. My approach allowed me to reduce the time spent on eating to boiling water in the morning for oatmeal and tea; everything else could be eaten cold. There would be no meal preparation and no substantial cleanup afterwards. The most important benefit of embracing the Spartan diet was that it lowered my pack weight by 23 pounds; a greater than 25% reduction in load. If practical, it would prove an impressive innovation.

Physically squared away and logistically sound, I had my gear selected and assembled to support 30 days alone in the field. I had a plan to reprovision that allowed me to double my time in the field. I had defined and acquired the food stuffs to meet the prescribed diet, and contingencies had been anticipated and accounted for. I had only to finalize the general route. Then I would load the gear and go.

Studying the maps of the upper half of SBW, I was excited to see it dotted with dozens of small alpine lakes. As I read articles and hikers' accounts of the area, I built up a list of things to see; 'Big Sand Lake', 'Hidden Lake', 'Moose Creek emptying into the Selway River'. As I circled those areas of interest on the map, a route began to take shape. The southern-most lake of interest to me was

Big Sand Lake which was just a few miles west-northwest of Blodgett Pass. I could reach Blodgett Pass and cross the Continental Divide by hiking 10 miles up Blodgett Canyon which was just a couple miles west of the town of Hamilton, Montana. My cousin would drive me to Hamilton and drop me at the trailhead of Blodgett Canyon. That would be the beginning of the trip. I would hike up Blodgett Canyon, cross the Continental Divide, drop into the Selway-Bitterroot Wilderness and head for Big Sand Lake.

For all of October, I would explore the Selway-Bitterroot by moving from lake to lake. I would work my way north as it suited me. With no rigid schedule, I could stop and enjoy the lakes and places I liked best and stay for as long as I liked. If weather came, I would welcome it. Time and any implied agenda became irrelevant. There was just one requirement; I needed to begin the Lolo Trail no later than November 1st. I had scouted a place where I could meet my cousin so I could reprovision between SBW and Lolo Trail. We worked out a code that I could broadcast using the Test function on my PLB. The code would let her know that I was two days away from our meeting point giving her time to respond by loading the truck and driving to meet me with much-needed provisions. With that plan in place and her invaluable support, I would be able to saunter through that vast wilderness alone for 30 days and up to another 30 days after reprovisioning. That would be all the time I would need to finish crossing the Rocky Mountains.

With all the logistics tended to and all my gear ready to be shipped to my cousin's house in Salmon, I was down to saying my goodbyes and cutting loose of my life. It had taken me much work on eBay and Craig's List, but I finally emptied a house full of crap and turned it into money for the next chapter of my life. So many things with which I had identified – gone. No longer a part of my life. No longer mine. At first, I felt a sense of loss. But after going through the process of selling off my life a piece at a time, I came to realize I was only selling stuff. It was mostly just stuff that I looked at or used to cover a blank spot on a wall. I actually picked up momentum after I sold the first few items; I went a little crazy in the effort to simplify my life. I sold all the DVDs I had collected over the years. I gave away recording equipment and things I thought meant a lot to me. I hauled carloads of clothes to the local donation bin. Then the day came when I realized a new definition of the word 'free' and a feeling like liberation washed over me. Without realizing it, I had completed one of the hardest parts of the trek before I even left town. I sold all my material possessions to buy the freedom I needed to follow adventure wherever it might take me.

I stored my car at my son's apartment complex. I left the access card to the storage facility with my remaining clothing and books in the car's console as well as one key to the storage lock. I kept the other key to the storage lock in my possession.

I moved my money to a single new account with a single debit card. I had the storage company draw off that card. I put my phone on Suspend so I could keep the number but would only pay a few dollars a month. There would be no texts or voice mails. I would be off the grid. Same thing with email; I left an auto-responder saying that I was gone on sabbatical with no anticipated time of return. I had vocationally, socially, and personally 'let go'.

At first, the reality of my dream coming to life was surreal. I had closed my businesses, sold nearly everything I owned, put my basics in a 10' x 10' storage shed, and told my family and closest friends not to have any expectations.

"Try not to have any expectations. I will call you when I can, but don't expect anything."

"What does that mean?" asked my youngest son, Dylan. "Like, ever?"

"Not 'ever', no. I'm sure I'll see you again, son, and I should be back pretty soon. I love you and always will. And I hope you contact me if you need help with something heavy. But don't expect me to be here on Thanksgiving or call on your birthday or to be around any time you need a couple dollars."

"No shit?"

"No shit. You're a man. You'll do better knowing you don't have a pillow to fall back on."

Dylan smiled even in the face of uncertainty. He was that way since he was a toddler, just naturally happy. And he totally loved his Dad.

"All right, man. I mean, I don't know what life will be without you. You've been right beside me all my life."

"I'll always be right beside you. I'm not leaving your life; I'm just leaving your days. You're busy anyway. You got this. And I'll be around. Just..."

"I know. I know. Don't have any expectations. From Dad. Shaking my head, man," he grinned and opened his long arms wide to hug me.

Strangely, I left his apartment second-guessing myself. Lulu (our family nickname for Dylan) was more than my youngest son; he was like a best friend to me and certainly a spirit with which I shared many lives. He spent more time camping with me than the other kids combined. After the divorce, his mother allowed him to live with me and finish high school in my care. Since he graduated, he had a plan for college and dreams that he was chasing, and I felt compelled to stay to lend a hand.

While I felt the tug on my heart when letting go of my children, I knew that they had their own lives and I could not live Life for them, no matter where I stayed. They had their own adventures to chase.

Perhaps the best thing I could do was show them that they could chase their dreams at any age and at any point in their lives as I had chosen to do.

I was not a part of that past anymore; that chapter of my life was closed. I created a new world for me. I never stopped loving anybody and never turned my back on family or friends, but I ruthlessly removed all limits on the adventure that was to be my new life.

Blodgett

After Brenda left me in the silence of the wild, I started my hike. Blodgett Canyon was the ideal entryway into what became the greatest trek of my life. It was long and lazy and mostly dark in the beginning. It was a deep canyon and fairly narrow so that the sun only got a few hours to nourish the life at its bottom. I made slow purposeful strides down the trail. I stretched my hamstrings under the load of my pack and exhaled the tension out of my neck, shoulders, and upper back. I had my trusty titanium hiking sticks that weighed 17 ounces as a pair; even when I wasn't actually using them for balance, they were great for keeping a rhythm or a pace. My sticks click-clicked deeper into the forest and alongside the creek that cut into the canyon.

Blodgett Creek ran along the south side of the canyon. It gurgled and purred and roared all along the 10-mile hike toward the mountain pass. The foliage came all the way up to my knees from the forest floor; the trail was draped with beautiful color that swished as I paced through it. The plants reached across the trail and were wet with dew that would have soaked my pants and filled my boots had I not worn my gaiters. It was almost like a jungle, especially after the first couple of miles. Lots of people came from town to enjoy a quick hike up Blodgett Canyon, but I could see where that activity ended. After passing the first few miles, the trail closed around me as a reminder that everything civilized was about to be left behind.

I gained elevation on the Blodgett Canyon Trail. I saw the change of season taking place in the canyon through which I passed. It lifted me. Starting the trek in October proved to be a great decision; there were no other human beings on the trail and I had the inspirational autumn colors to myself. I caught the mountain range between seasons. I looked and listened to the natural vista around me and I felt that my timing was good.

As I traveled up the canyon, I came upon a lovely little camping spot that sat in a bend in the creek. There were several likely fishing holes within easy walk of the site. I decided to call an end to the first day and set up camp. Expedition packs had somewhat elaborate suspension systems, so I had to unbuckle a few straps before I could slide the black pack off my shoulders to the ground. It had a long pocket on the front and a bottom compartment that zippered open from the main body of the pack for easy access to equipment. All its zippers were water-sealed. I grabbed my tent from the bottom section and the two lightweight poles from the long front pocket. I shook the tent out over the flattest piece of ground I could find and slipped the two poles into sleeves that crossed the tent – one near the bottom and a longer one near the top – and that raised the tent and fly. Then I nailed the narrow bottom in with two stakes, each stake the size of a 6" long pencil, walked around to the front of the tent, pulled it snug, and nailed it tight. The result was a long red half-used tube of toothpaste. The flattened end faced into the wind, redirecting it over and around the tent opening on the other end, giving the tube tent a wind rating in excess of 80 mph. It had a tub bottom, adjustable ventilation, and a vestibule for cooking and stowing gear. I snugged up the adjustment straps and opened up the door. Then I turned to the pack and started stowing gear.

I placed a self-inflating air mattress down the center of the floor and laid the sleeping bag out on the mattress. On the left (looking in) went the journal, Big Thump (my bear pistol), and the water bottle. On the right were my clothing and my possibles bag. I stored the pack in the right side of the vestibule and stowed the stove to the left. Waterproof food bags were hung in a tree not too far from camp.

Once camp was established, the serious relaxation began.

"Breathe deep and relax," I reminded myself. "For cryin' out loud, Taylor; you're all alone for the foreseeable future. Nowhere to be; no one to call. Just settle your big self down and relax." Then I smiled at myself and laughed a little. Over time, it became a mantra for the trek.

"Just settle your big self down…"

Some say nothing is more relaxing than fishing, so I took my lightweight fishing gear off the outside of the pack. I kept a small assortment of lures in a plastic box in the top pocket of the pack. One had a hook with black and pink feathers, and it was love at first sight.

I was not a great fisherman, but it seemed like a good way to supplement my sparse meal plan and a great way to pass the time. Moreover, the Selway was well-known for the mountain lakes I would be visiting on my trip and they were part of the criteria used for defining the first half of my trek. I tied the lucky lure on the line of my Dad's pole. I was such a lame excuse for a fisherman that I didn't even own my own pole.

Casually, I tossed the lure out in the creek. I reeled it in, stiffly, to be honest; it took a while to get my fishing groove on. I tossed it back to the same spot and reeled it in again. A total of six times; that was a rule I had just made up. There was no logic to the number; it was totally random. But I decided I would make it a tradition and, from that moment on, I cast six times at each targeted spot and no more. I moved up the creek with the black/pink featherette and tossed it with great confidence to a new "lucky spot". I hooked one on the fifth cast. The backcountry fishing rod and reel was very lightweight and I didn't know what to expect, but it pulled the little fish through the water back to me. That black/pink featherette proved an irresistible color combination to the fish in that part of the wilderness. I released about a half dozen before I thought about saving one for dinner. The next good sized catch got flipped up on to the log on the bank where I brained him with Big Thump. I didn't shoot him; I just dropped the weight of that big cylinder down on the fish's head and thump! A quick merciful end; no flipping or flopping. Fresh fish for dinner.

I needed to cook the fish before it got dark so I went to get my possibles bag out of the tent. The term 'possibles' comes from 18th century trappers. It refers to a bag or a satchel in which they would carry everything they would possibly need in a day. My possibles bag was made of dark orange, almost brown, rip-stop nylon and was about as big as an old-fashioned oatmeal carton. In it, I carried a first aid/repair kit, a tourniquet, a fire kit, compass, headlamps, and a Leatherman. I grabbed the fire kit and the Leatherman and tossed the possibles back into the tent.

It didn't take long to gather wood because I rarely built big fires. Big fires left big messes and Dad taught us to Leave No Trace. I found a large stone, turned it over, and built a fire in its mark. When finished with the fire, I scattered the few ashes and turned the stone back over the scar leaving the campsite the way I found it. After quickly gathering an armload of wood, I built a small teepee of kindling, lit a piece of pitchwood with my lighter, and slipped the firestarter into the teepee. Pitchwood was the coolest thing ever to share with people who were new to the forest. Essentially, it was wood that was heavily and naturally infused with pitch, which made it very flammable and easy to light. Pitchwood had the kindling teepee burning in a matter of seconds and I slowly added more fuel to the flames. It was my habit to burn wood 'Indian-style' where sticks and logs were burned on the end, turned in to a fire like spokes on a wheel where the fire was the hub, as opposed to crossing or piling wood and spreading ashes over a larger areas. While I fed the fire, I carved a smoking stick for the fish. It had to be about four feet long and thick enough to go straight through the lower back but thin enough not to do too much damage. I whittled small pegs to pin the fish side-to-side to keep it on the smoking stick. I positioned stones to hold the fish over the coals at the right height while I relaxed and watched it cook.

My mind was not yet quiet, but I felt some depth in my thinking. No longer strapped to the superficial clutter that I left behind, I began to slow down and think deeper. I closed my eyes and sat in natural meditation; expanded my senses of smelling and hearing. I sniffed the smoke from the fire. As my awareness increased, I could smell the fish roasting separate from the smell of the smoke. I even picked out the smell of the raw fish as the smoke first rolled over it and wafted it towards me. At the same time, my sense of hearing expanded dramatically. It was my favorite of the five senses; partially because it was my best developed sense and partially because it was so powerful. I felt that – in the wilderness – I could hear further than I could see. I heard the wind pass through the canyon above me. I heard it tickle the tall grass that grew in the open spaces. I felt the wilder side of me waking up.

I sat on my heels and watched the smoke rise up and around the fish-on-a-stick. I had stripped down to my blue base layer and was barefoot. I lifted the smoking stick from the fire, let it cool for a few minutes, and flaked the tender succulent meat off the bone. It was, in a sense, primal. I was becoming a part of my surroundings. I would continue to grow more instinctual, but I had settled into the trek. After finishing the fish, I threw the bone in the fire along with the smoking sticks and watched them burn down to dust.

When I went to bed, I stowed my boots in the vestibule, tossed my clothing to one side, and slipped into the VBL in my bag wearing only my skivvies. A BVBL - or Vapor Barrier Liner – was like a body condom that lined the sleeping bag and kept perspiration from getting caught up in it's down filler. Over time, the accumulation of perspiration in down could dramatically compromise the bag's temperature rating. It was not important on short trips, but VBL use was recommended on extended cold weather treks to keep a sleeping bag dry and warm. The combination of bag, VBL, and mattress would keep me warm to -20 degrees. Any colder than that and I would have to sleep in my long johns. I placed my socks and base layer clothing inside at the bottom of my bag so they would be warm in the morning. I kept all the really dirty stuff in the vestibule and all my clean stuff inside. I unzipped the door to my tent and dropped on all fours to pass through the vestibule. I zipped up the flaps as I crawled into my tent, slid into the VBL and bag, and slipped off to sleep about 8 o'clock that night.

I awoke almost ten hours later and lay still in the comfort of my sleeping bag. There was no schedule to keep, no reason to hurry. I listened to the water tumbling down the creek and the sounds of birds in the trees all around me. I stretched my arms above my head and my long body through the tent. I unzipped the bag so my bare skin could acclimate to the cool autumn temperatures. I listened to the wind to measure its mood. As I came fully awake, I visualized my climb over Blodgett Pass.

I imagined the view changing with every few hundred feet of elevation gained. As the altitude increased, so would my field of view down the 10-mile canyon. I could almost see the fall palette of color increasing; a virtual river of tall pines flowing down a canyon formed by towering granite faces and all the space between the trees and the peaks swirling in every shade of yellow, orange, red, rust, and green. As I moved up the switchbacks toward the pass, the wind would increase in speed and the temperature would get lower. Even though I had officially passed into the Selway-Bitterroot Wilderness a couple miles back, I expected the trail up to the pass to be well-maintained to the top; it was a well-traveled path in the summer months. However, I did not know what to expect on the other side of the ridge; only that it would be steep and untamed and vast.

A slow surge of excitement coursed through me, so I sat up and peeled the VBL off to get ready for my day. Clammy bastards, those VBLs; like sleeping in a dry cleaning bag. I removed it inside/out and tossed it to the grass to air out. I pulled my socks and long johns from the bottom of my bag and put the top and socks on. I wouldn't need the bottoms; with all the work planned for that day, my legs wouldn't get too cold. I grabbed the water bottle and stove, slipped my feet into my boots, and stood tall as soon as I exited the tent. I stretched my back out as I stood on my toes and reached up into the western sky. With a couple deep breaths, I hooked my muscles up to my brain and did an inventory of important things:

1. Temperature

2. Precipitation

3. Immediate Danger

4. Discomfort/Pain

At number four, I realized I needed to relieve myself, so I went to water the bushes. Upon my return, I assembled the stove.

The manufacturer of my backpacking stove engineered it to boil water fast. That's all it was good for; full throttle or nothing. No simmering food with that stove. The idea was that boiling water was all a backpacker needed for freeze dried foods and tea. The faster water was boiled, the more efficient the use of fuel. I liked it because it broke down into a real space-saving package, plus I needed the larger capacity pot for melting snow and ice for drinking water. I pulled my Reactor from its stuff sack and removed the clear plastic lid. Nestled inside were the fuel canister (about the size of tall round Cinnabon) and the heating element. I removed them, screwed the heating element on to the fuel canister, turned the valve and lit the stove. It roared to life and heat raced through metal channels when I laid the turbine-shaped bottom of the pot directly on the heater. In the same stuff sack, I carried a titanium spork (combination spoon/fork), a small titanium cup, and a Ziploc full of my favorite cinnamon orange tea.

I laid the items out on the ground by the stove and ran off to fetch the food bags from the tree. One was purple and the other was teal. I pulled on the quick release knot on the hanging line and lowered the bags from their safe place. I took the gallon Ziploc bag of oatmeal out, filled my small cup about 1/3 full, and poured boiling hot water into the cup. I turned the stove off and held the cup in my hands.

It wasn't a cold morning, but autumn was in the air. It was crisp. Cool. Some might think it cold. The thin titanium cup conducted heat from the water into my hands and it felt good. I rolled it around and inhaled its flavor through my nose. I looked at it. With water added, the cooked oatmeal halfway filled my cup. A little more, maybe. A little more than half a cup. And it was good; maple and brown sugar flavor. I ate every spoonful, then cleaned it with a licky finger. I refilled the cup with hot water from the stove and dropped a teabag into it. I might as well have been a Tibetan monk performing some sacred ritual for all the time I was taking with breakfast. I slipped my windskins on, lightweight windproof trekking pants, and opted for a sweater instead of a jacket. The tea was memorable. It had long been a favorite of mine, but never better than on the day I was to cross Blodgett Pass.

I put the double-snug on my B-52s. As I testified in journal entries, articles, and in person, those Salomon mountaineering boots were the finest piece of gear I ever owned. Lightweight at 22 ounces but with a rugged, flexible grip for long hikes and rock hopping across creeks and stiff edges for side hilling. Warm and waterproof. I had a set of microspikes that I could attach in an instant that made the boots all but slip-proof on the ice. Since purchasing the B-52s, I had fallen through frozen creeks, powered through deep powder, traversed exposed ledges, and raced through creek crossings that filled them with water; they were the best alpine climbing boots I ever owned. They felt like armor. After putting a double knot in the laces, I stretched my feet inside the boots and wrapped my gaiters around my calves to cover my lower legs. I was dressed, but not ready to go.

My camp was organized such that breaking it down was the reverse of setting it up. The items were loaded into the pack with the stove and tea on top of the upper section for easy access during breaks. After being emptied of its contents, I rolled the tent up and placed in the bottom compartment of the pack. The tent poles were pushed into the long front pocket which also held my Gore-Tex shell. I rolled my fire rock back into position to cover any trace of my small fish fire. I strapped on Big Thump which rode in a custom leather sling holster positioned in the center of my chest. I surveyed the area to make sure there was no visible trace of my visit. When satisfied with the cleanup, I reached down to pick up my pack.

"Damn, you're heavy," I said out loud as I slung the load up on my shoulders. It took as much timing as it did strength. I knew that the pack would literally get lighter every day and that I would grow stronger every day, but it sure felt heavy that morning knowing where I was going. I leaned over and bucked the pack up onto my back and fastened the hip belt tight before I stood tall. With the weight on my hips, I tightened the shoulder straps enough to keep the load steady. I grabbed my sticks, looked over the site one final time, and took off up the trail to the crossing.

Physically, I felt my body was acclimating to the high country quickly. I felt the separation in my quadriceps and I put extra pressure on my toes to stretch and strengthen my calves. I had spent the last five years bodybuilding or working in gyms so I was physically strong enough for the trek, but bench presses and squats weren't the same kind of exercise as backpacking and climbing so my muscles had to adjust. I took pleasure in their responsiveness as I spent that morning's first hour hiking to the base of the climb.

Mentally, I shook off the detritus of my civilized life. I literally carried everything I needed to live on my back. I was as free as a man could be in modern times. In the dark forgotten corners of my mind, I knew that the trek would end and, in some form or fashion, I would return to the toxic bullshit of the Real World. But I forced those thoughts away and cordoned them off from my present reality. I pretended to be an angel-in-training doing some reconnaissance for God in another possible Garden of Eden… checking it out and marking a trail for those human beings to follow.

I loved to take my brain off the leash and set it free to think where it was inclined to go. Unconventional by nature, I was free to express my most extreme self to my heart and soul's content in the backcountry. As loud and crude or melodic and tranquil as I chose, there was no peer or social pressure to influence my behavior. I could be a poet lying in fields of gold or a barbarian lording over his domain. I was a 58-year old boy in the biggest playground you can imagine without the burden of adult supervision.

Less than two miles from the last camp, I spotted switchbacks on the hillside to my right. Most creatures climbed a hill by going side-to-side; rather than climb straight up a slope, man and animals tended to go uphill diagonally. A climber switches back and forth as he travels uphill, making the climb a little bit longer and a little easier, as well. I stopped and studied the switchbacks. I looked up the path for the pass hoping to see the destination from where I stood on the trail. Seeing only mountainside, I knew that it would be many hours before I saw the pass, but I felt certain I would see it that day.

As I turned up the switchbacks leading to Blodgett Pass, I compensated for changes in the physical dynamics of the hike. As the trail got steeper and more narrow, it required me to shift the weight of my cargo as well as shorten my stride. The incline asked my toes to grab and climb the trail, but my glutes and hamstrings wanted me to push off my heels. My sticks took on a more important role when maneuvering around small obstacles and keeping balance on the slope. My lungs pumped like the bellows of an angry blacksmith by the time I reached the third switchback. The trail diminished in quality; it was still well-traveled but not well-maintained. A fallen tree or talus from a slide made the climb more interesting as I got higher. The trail and pass had been closed from 2011-2012 and only reopened after a great deal of trail clearing by the Forest Service and local volunteers.

At a turn, I stopped to catch my breath. I looked back down the canyon I had travelled and was enthralled by the higher perspective. The decomposing granite mountains stood like fluted towers on either side of the canyon. They were a gray-blue color and took on a chalky hue when struck by the sun. Above them, the blue sky was textured with clouds too thin to be called cotton. More like lint.

"Gossamer," I concluded out loud to nobody there.

The mountains turned to boulders turned to rocks piled up at the bottom. But the bottom was obscured from view on the trail. The forest helped sift the rocks into sand that would continue its migration down Blodgett Creek and hid the rocks from hikers on the trail. From where I stood on the side of the mountain, I saw the talus slopes emptying out near the bottom of the canyon. I noticed how the forest thinned out around me and how much closer were the snow-capped peaks of the Bitterroots. I stood up against the pack straps and absorbed the weight of the load. I flexed my legs, tightened my core, and pointed my way toward the pass.

Twice I thought I saw the pass ahead. Twice, I was fooled by rocks and trees. I anticipated a passageway with few trees and a spectacular view of the Rocky Mountains, but the pass was below tree line so there wouldn't be a windswept saddle. I stopped at every switchback to rest. It would be overly dramatic to call it a grueling climb, but it was more than a thousand feet up a pretty steep mountain with a 60 pound pack on my back. And then, almost surprising me, it was there.

Blodgett Pass. I stepped into Idaho as I departed Montana. The view was from an ancient world. Sheer faces of granite formed a seven mile crescent-shaped wall that started on my right and bent toward the left-middle of the view. The continuous ridgeline called to me, seemed to me a lure. It bent toward Big Sand Lake, the next point on my map. I tried to visualize the location of the lake; moving left off the point of the crescent, Blodgett Mountain and Shattuck Mountain came into view. They framed the left side, their light-colored rock streaked with dark rock here and there. Between the massifs and the crescent wall, trees filled in the void and seemed to flow down from the mountains like a river. Firs and Ponderosa pines, tamarack, and scrub mottled the landscape with every shade of gold and red and green. From where I stood on the pass looking down on the Selway-Bitterroot Wilderness, the world seemed so much larger. I couldn't travel in a day as far as I could see. And I was traveling to a place many horizons away. For me, the real adventure began at the pass. That's where I literally stepped off the edge.

I paused at the pass, took a picture to document location and date, and fired up the stove to brew a cup of tea. There were lots of great rocks to perch in on the pass and I found one that blocked the wind without blocking the view. I took everything in while taking a break and that's when I noticed the change.

I had been listening to the layers of wind. There was the great big wind that scoured the peaks; that was one that everyone could hear. There was a lighter wind that rolled down the rocks and mixed with leaves to rustle and make other layers of sound. And that wind stopped blowing. It seemed like everything stopped. One moment, I was listening to the surround sound of Nature and the next, silence. I felt a presence. Nothing to be scared of but something unusual. Like something watching me.

I rose from the rocks to have a look around; slowly, smoothly, and without sound. I felt the presence on my right but it was outside my peripheral vision. I turned as slow as syrup to see what was putting out such a tangible vibe. Standing 10' above me and 50' away, the most bright white mountain goat stood calmly watching me. He was extraordinary. He seemed huge; they ranged from 100 to maybe 300 pounds. He seemed a little on the big side; about the size of a Salmon River black bear which made him a damn big mountain goat. He was radiant; shimmering on the top of a rock at the top of a mountain ridgeline. We made eye contact. I tried not to blink. He was easy to look into; a shaman who had nothing to fear from me. His horns curved slightly and were twice as long as his ears. His coat was full in anticipation of winter, but his lower legs had less hair. It looked like he was wearing plus-fours. He stood on top of the rocks with green pine trees all around and one dead gray one curving up behind the creature. He did not move at all; for a moment, I thought he might have been a product of my imagination.

I stood mesmerized by the mountain goat. I knew what it meant as a symbol to the people native to that area; it symbolized independence. Distance and space. Not anti-social, necessarily; just independent. Spiritually, it encouraged individual adventure for the sole purpose of individual knowing. Its love of heights symbolized spiritual ambition. It climbed which represented progress and achievement. And there he stood on the precipice with ease. I couldn't believe the serendipity of the scene; it seemed staged. His oversized cloven hooves didn't move as the wind blew through his thick white coat. The mountain goat seemed inanimate. Neither his head nor his ears moved, but he looked me over and I waited for some feedback. Without fanfare, he left as silently and surprisingly as he arrived. I stood on an empty spot in time and basked in the afterglow of a spiritual climax.

From my position, the mountains defended the horizon in every direction. They were immense. Seemingly impenetrable. As the larger view enveloped me, I thought of Lewis at the top of the Continental Divide. At Lemhi Pass, a little less than 140 miles south of where I crossed, Meriwether Lewis first gazed out on the Rockies. I tried to channel his anxiety, his sense of urgency, and I felt his pulse quicken. Meriwether Lewis had to succeed; somehow they had to cross the boundless mountains. All of them. And they reached further than the eye could see. I looked to the crescent wall of mountains below me, tried to measure it and match it with a time, and used that as a measuring stick to 'guesstimate' some distances toward the horizon. I was amazed at how far I had to go. In fact, it was better not to think of it; better to take it just one camp at a time.

Those first few days on the trail were a time of great transition. There were adjustments to be made; changes in diet, exercise patterns, and sleep cycles that required substantial changes in my thinking and doing. I spent a couple of days working the kinks out of my gear management routines. Initially, I didn't care about my pace or the number of miles covered; I knew, in the long run, it was more important to start out right than to start out fast. There were things that didn't hang quite right or that were used more often than expected. I had to get used to carrying a pack again. I carried the same expedition pack for years and its aluminum stays were custom-curved for my body. In spite of that, it took a couple days on the trail for my body and pack to merge into a single working unit. During that break-in time, I constantly fumbled with and adjusted straps to obtain a better fit or a better balance for the load. It took days for me to adjust to not thinking about food. I knew I had enough food for the trip but, being a Texan, I suffered withdrawals from hot bread, sweet tea, and pork ribs. Instead of those luxurious foods, I drank a protein shake after humping a pack through the wilderness all day and ate a pouch of tuna in the evening. I didn't try to catch fish very often, so the pouch of tuna became my catch-of-the-day. I adjusted to the new normal and I felt there was something symbolic about it. I remember being amused at how easily I could adjust to such a dramatic change in physical environment and lifestyle, yet struggle sorely with relatively simple problems back home.

The Idaho territory was new to me but not the activity. I started climbing in my early twenties and began diving into serious adventure as I neared thirty. Before I became stuck under the Wheel of Life, I was an avid adventurer. I climbed vertical rock and ice, and enjoyed long alpine climbs on our continent and others. I hiked literally all over the world in every climate imaginable; in the desert sands of the Middle East, the jungles of Borneo and Indonesia, across glaciers and along the spines of some of the highest mountain ranges in the world. I began soloing when I could no longer find partners for my adventures. There was no reason to believe that the Idaho trek was beyond my capabilities except that I was going so deep for so long. But I wanted the trip to take me far away and last a long time; my real challenge was navigating a vast new territory.

Winter was just around the corner and winter was a bad time to get lost in a million acre wilderness.

I focused on doing all the little things during those first few days. I purposely took a great deal of time to do them and things smoothed out as I made adjustments. My bones began to bend better and my joints flexed easier; I sat on my heels instead of logs and rocks. I stopped thinking about emails and my old life, and I watched the sky all day. I listened to the prevailing wind and practiced primitive navigation. Knowing the wind usually came from the northwest allowed me to navigate crudely with my face; as long as the wind was striking me on my left cheek, I moved in the right direction -a due north. I emptied the air from my belly and breathed in deeply, sampling the smells as I inhaled. I tried to visualize the smells… to make them two or three-dimensional. I got used to looking in the distance again. I practiced using my peripheral vision and not looking at the trail every step. I lengthened my stride, which was considerable, and found the rhythm that allowed me to cover a lot of ground. The thought-storms that plagued me subsided somewhat as I immersed myself in the ultimate distraction. I focused on the basics and took time to do them right. It was a critical step towards making the transition from a scattered city dweller to an attentive mountain man.

I gathered up my gear and headed down into the Selway. It was a great moment on the trek; dropping off the pass and into the wilderness. Utterly alone for the next 30 days in the literal middle of nowhere. The trail took me down steep switchbacks through the pines. It did not follow the ridge. The motion dynamics changed suddenly and dramatically as I headed downhill with the pack. My knees and quadriceps took the brunt of the impact. I used my sticks to help pull me up the hill on the climb, but they were mostly used for timing and balance on the descent. Similarly, my lungs pumped hard on the climb but were nearly idle on the way down. I consciously held my momentum in check; I did not want to speed down the hill. I wanted to take my time looking down into the Selway. It was a view I might never take in again. I put the brakes on and shortened my stride. I set an appropriate pace. I thought of John Muir, the patron saint of 20th century environmentalism and the founder of the Sierra Club, and his opinion on wilderness travel:

> "Hiking - I don't like either the word or the thing. People ought to saunter in the mountains - not hike! Do you know the origin of that word 'saunter'? It's a beautiful word. Away back in the Middle Ages, people used to go on pilgrimages to the Holy Land. And when people in the villages through which they passed asked where they were going, they would reply, 'A la sainte terre,' - 'To the Holy Land.' And so they became known as sainte-terre-ers or saunterers. Now these mountains are our Holy Land, and we ought to saunter through them reverently, not 'hike' through them."
> ~ John Muir (1838 -1914)

"A la sainte terre", I said aloud as I became fully absorbed by my surroundings. I emptied my lungs all the way to the bottom, forced every stale pocket to give up its dust, and filled myself with air that was as refreshing to breathe as the cold mountain water was to drink. I cycled my lungs again, released tension, and slowed down. I rode my body down the hill. I sauntered through the undergrowth that carpeted an opening in the rocks and trees as the slope became more gradual. I looked around the crescent, I felt about halfway down the face and the terrain was less steep. Clumps of tall wild grass – green with white wheaty tips – contrasted beautifully with the green bushes that looked like someone has splashed them with red dots from a small paintbrush. As though the color change was a disease, the red spread out from the dot to take the rest of the green leaves on the bush into fall. It was mostly green trees, golden brown shrubs, splashes of red, and an occasional silvery gray boulder. My eyes lost their restrictive focus and gathered beauty from the peripheral limits of my sight. I had adjusted to see better the entirety of the panorama. The Great Bigness of it all seemed infinite, laid out before me like a banquet of beautiful things. In that moment, I forgot about the weight of the pack, my aching legs, the wild trail. I almost forgot about myself. It was a treasured moment of backcountry bliss.

For the rest of the day, I let my body do its own thinking. I knew where Big Sand Lake was or at least its general direction. I knew how the sun moved in the sky and where on my face to keep the wind. I didn't have to think; I could instead rely on instinct. It wasn't easy, but I practiced until I got used to it. Switching to Observation Mode, I watched the sky and smelled the air for any change in the weather as I strode down the trail. I stayed alert, in the moment, and moved with confidence as I leaned into my stride. It was important to pay attention and avoid injuries that could become major problems in the backcountry, and I had to stay on course and navigate with or without a trail to guide me. But I didn't have to think to do those things. My body and brain could manage it for me.

In a matter of days, my brain had gone from a rolling boil of thoughts and flashes and bursts of energy to a slow and easy simmer. Thoughts still bubbled up, but there were fewer of them and there was less turmoil. I had the time mentally to play with things, to see them more clearly as I rolled them around. Things like songs or situations or relationships or poems. I thought about one poem all day. Nothing to be concerned with but that poem and what it meant to me. I had the luxury of watching its meaning change as I applied it to different incidents or events in my life. Oh, the pleasure of epiphany when the Bell of Truth would ring.

A poem by Kipling kept me company for miles. My grandmother made me memorize it when I was ten years old. She gave me a book of poems for Christmas in 1966 and I had to memorize a new poem every week to recite for her on Saturdays.

"If you can make one heap of all your winnings
And risk it at one turn of pitch-and-toss
And lose, and start again at the beginning
And never breathe a word about your loss."

"If" by Rudyard Kipling was a poem that defined much of the criteria for manhood, as a father might explain it to a son. While I strolled on the trail, the words came to me clearly, effortlessly, even after the passage of so much time. Every verse appeared as if set free from some locked corner in my mind and I played with the words for a while. Grandma would have loved it. The poem's lesson meant something different to me then than it did when I was ten. Ironic, really, that I committed it to memory so early but waited so late to appreciate its wise guidance.

I stopped in the late afternoon to set up camp. It had been a good day and I wanted to stay high enough on the slope to keep the horizon in the distance. To watch the sun set over the Rockies. I found water, dropped my pack, and had the tent raised in a couple of minutes. Then I mixed up my protein drink and sat back for the rest of the day.

All I did for the rest of the evening was listen; I made no noise but for the sound of my breathing and drinking. Likewise, there was little in the way of sound coming from the Selway. A grouse came by one side of the camp, strutting with his neck extending on the pause between every step. It seemed territorial; he didn't have that courtship vibe. I looked past the feathered sentry to see into the woods for something else. Not the mountain goat; he was up higher. But something that might be the cause of the tangible quiet – something like a moose. Moose were in rut in October and become dangerously aggressive. They were enormous animals and could strike out with their front hooves hard enough to kill a human. I was taught to get behind a tree if ever I encountered one in rut and keep the tree between us or the moose might stomp me to death. It might have been a moose putting everyone on edge, or just a very quiet evening. The harder I listened, the quieter it seemed. Even the wind was holding its breath.

"That's the thing about the wilderness," I remembered as I listened expectantly. "You never know what is going to happen."

I broke the nervous silence with an explosion of pent-up laughter. Laughing out loud for no apparent reason; it was the first time and I soon learned it was one of the greatest things about being alone in the wilderness. I could laugh at anything that struck me as funny. Seriousness was replaced with spontaneous glee. I laughed out loud often. Alone in the backcountry was a happy place for me.

Big Sand

Becoming a part of the truly natural world meant becoming a part of the food chain. In the remote regions of North America (Idaho/Montana/Wyoming), Mankind technically fell a few links down the food chain because mountain lions, grizzly bears, and wolves inhabited the region and were potential predators of Man. Lions and wolves rarely attacked human beings, but grizzly bears were an authentic danger. They killed hunters, hikers, and outdoor enthusiasts every year. On average, they weighed 600-800 pounds, had 4" claws, and could run as fast as 35 miles per hour. I encountered two of them during a lifetime in the mountains.

The first grizzly bear I saw up close was mostly a blur. It was hunkered over eating grasshoppers on a hillside and I was downwind on the other side when I crested the small ridge between us. I was shocked to see it there and it was equally surprised to see me. It looked six feet tall bent over. It snorted and got bigger and taller as it stood and turned to check me out. But it didn't get a good look at me; I was gone by the time he completed his turn. I was taught not to run from bears, but never bought into that bullshit. Maybe if a person was fat or wearing slippers or otherwise handicapped, but that rule didn't apply to me. That bear might have smelled me, but he damned sure didn't see me; just something blurry like a monkey with a backpack running down the hill, mouth open as if screaming but no sound coming out.

The second grizzly bear I encountered was even scarier than the first. He rose up from the willows by the creek I was crossing. Willows along a creek are despicably good cover for bears and I should have been more alert for him. I should have avoided the willows altogether. He started out massive and got bigger as he came to full height. He looked like a big hairy backhoe with teeth. Like a good Marine, I fell back on my training. I tried to look large by standing tall and spreading my arms out, and I recall growling ridiculously in a deep scare-the-bear voice. He might have been amused, but he looked pissed. Then he roared. I thought briefly about shooting at him, but instead soiled my trousers while I ran. There were too many grizzly bears in Montana and Wyoming; that's one reason I was trekking in Idaho.

All joking aside, a wise mountaineer must be prepared for the possibility of a bear attack. Some hikers wear bells and hunters often carry pepper spray as a repellent. After the grizzly experiences in Wyoming, it became my habit to carry 'bear medicine'; a Smith & Wesson Model 500 .50 magnum pistol loaded with 440 grain bullets. It was like shooting a lead-filled beer can. I called the weapon Big Thump and never went backcountry without it. Thump was unique in mission and design. Smith and Wesson had to develop an entirely new frame, the X-frame, to handle the sheer power generated by the oversized bullets and magnum charge. The cylinder held only five rounds instead of the usual six in revolvers. Basically, the six-shooter gave up a shot for all that extra power. It had a muzzle break to help reduce the recoil but was still too much for many people. Unlike first generation hand cannons, however, the Model 500 didn't wrench the wrist. Its superior engineering directed the recoil straight back through the frame and into the pad between the shooter's forefinger and thumb on the palm of his hand. When I shot Big Thump, I kept my hands firm not tight around the weapon and my arms loose; as they absorbed the recoil from a shot, they lifted my hands up to where I could see under them. If I tried to hold him down, sooner or later Thump would bite. It was a bit of a bother, but Thump was the perfect solution for grizzlies. I learned mountaineering in Wyoming and started soloing there, and parts of Wyoming provided a protected habitat for grizzly bears. Consequently, in the areas around Yellowstone Park toward Cody, they were as thick as fleas on a dog. The bad thing about grizzly bears was that they eat you to death. Big Thump was the equalizer; predators were less of a concern. With Big Thump in my hand, I moved back to the top of the food chain.

The protein drink I sipped on that afternoon was luxurious. I got 240 important calories after finishing a day's hike. It was like a Creamsicle, a delicious orange ice cream bar that we used to eat when I was a kid. All I had to do was use my water filter pump to draw water from a source into my water bottle. I could get about a quart of snowy cold fresh water into the bottle. I would fill it halfway and put a couple of scoops of the protein powder into it, shake it hard for half a minute, and enjoy a foamy orange milkshake that quickly fed my tired muscles and met my need for something sweet. It broke down better than other powders; there were no lumps and the taste was superior. I had oatmeal in the morning, and jerky and trail mix during the day. After I set up camp, I had protein and rebuilt my muscles. It was a treat, to be sure.

Between sips, I planned my approach to Big Sand Lake. I had maps downloaded to my GPS, but the screen was small. I preferred traditional topographical maps for route planning and path finding. Those are the kind used by my father, the kind of maps I've used my entire life, and I had two of those for the Selway as well as the Lewis & Clark trail. I laid out the topos, took a big drink of protein, and got on my hands and knees to look over the maps.

Big Sand Lake was an easy hike from where I was camped. It was less than a full day's hike away and there did not appear to be any considerable changes in elevation once I reached the base of the crescent ridge. It appeared that I could sleep late in the morning and still have time to complete the hike to Big Sand the next day. It made me smile because Big Sand seemed to set the pace for the entire trip through the Selway. For the most part, I planned to travel a few miles at a time until I found someplace cool to call home. I might stay overnight or for a few days. When it got later in the month and I moved further north to the Lolo Trail, I would have to push it harder. But during October while deep in the Selway, I didn't have to push it at all. I could hear Muir's words in my head and smiled at his contribution to the next day's plans.

"I'll just saunter on to Big Sand Lake when I feel like getting up," I declared as I sat up on my heels from the map and lifted my chin high to drain the last delectable drops of creamy orange goodness from my water bottle. "And I think I'll get up... uhh, when I can't sleep anymore!"

I laughed out loud. When the echoes died, I sat in the quiet with a Cheshire grin on my face. I was getting used to my newfound freedom. I balanced in my squat and thought about nothing-in-particular.

Thoughts bubbled up in the quiet. I tried to let them pass unnoticed, hoping to ignore them until they popped and drifted off. Some were random, the by-product of the mental cleansing that resulted from spending time in the wild, but some were meaningful and difficult to ignore. Thoughts of my children were the hardest to let go. And thoughts of plans failed or efforts wasted were unwanted but clung like burrs to my consciousness. I was learning that airing out my mind was like drying out my boots; I had to leave it open if all that funky stuff was to escape. Abstract out-of-nowhere images from some of the landmarks in my life. It struck me as odd that the memorable moments of our lives – the parties and celebrations and the toasts made to commemorate those moments – were not, in fact, memories that lived on without maintenance. Those great moments were no different than the worst moments in that we only remembered them if we tried. I sampled the truth in that thought, and then it rose like smoke and was gone. I practiced letting thoughts slip away and saved my energy for important ones.

My eyes adjusted to the darkness as the sun went down. Since I was spiking out in a temporary trail camp, I made no fire. My vision was optimized for the dark. I pulled off my boots, slipped into my tent booties, put on my down jacket and stayed out in the night. As the world turned and the sun moved away toward the Pacific Ocean, the absence of light allowed me to see the stars as few people in the city could see them.

I have lived in cities around the world and I've seen stars from all of them, but the cities' night skies were filled with light that attenuated the sparkling of the stars. Only the brightest stars could be seen from a city. From where I sat in the Selway-Bitterroot Wilderness, I could see a sky full of stars that filled the sea of night; stars with clarity and color I didn't know could be seen with the naked eye. I felt that I could crudely discern stars closer than others, some stars being brighter or smaller or more colorful. I could see the Milky Way. As one who practiced primal navigation, the stars were an important tool to me; not as a real-time trailblazing tool but a tried-and-true method of checking one's bearings after the sun went down. If I made camp and the Dipper was on my forward right at night, then I was heading in the right direction. I knew where to find the Big Dipper and I knew to follow the line formed by the leading edge upwards to find the North Star. I knew that those constellations retained their positions relative to one another and that they shifted their position in the sky as weeks went by. I watched them every night that the sky allowed it while on the trek; I knew right where they would be. As I looked up at the North Star, then down and a little left, I imagined my track along the edge of the forest about a mile from the end of the ridge. I looked back up at the Dipper and smiled at how easy it was to see; so many constellations with names that make no sense, but the Big Dipper looked exactly like a great big dipper in the sky. Basic instincts were awakened with just a little practice. I put my hands above my head and stretched out against a rock. I took a deep breath and exhaled knots and tight spots and kinks from my trusty old body. I lifted my butt off the ground and tried to loosen my old shoulders in the stretch. I felt strong. It had been an exceptional day and, hopefully, I would grow stronger every day. My brain reminded me that I needed to be strong and prepared for the unexpected as there was plenty of that ahead.

One of the great things about camping in the late fall and winter were the long nights. In October, it got dark before 6 o'clock in the Selway. As the trek progressed into the later stages, I set up camps at 3 p.m. because it got dark at 4 o'clock. So, in the Selway, the sun went down and I ate my pouch of tuna. I sat around for a while to watch the stars when it got good and dark. Maybe journal with a headlamp for an hour or so. And after all that, it was still only eight o'clock. I could sleep twelve hours and be up by 8 a.m.! Awesome. Just awesome. I was going to practice sleeping a lot. I stowed my gear and slid into my bag.

I woke up not knowing when or where I was but remembered a dream about eating hot buttered bread. It may have been a lucid dream because I languished in it for a while. Then I laid on my side using my jacket for a pillow and listened without moving in the dark because I realized a whuump had woken me.

Whuump.

It was a familiar sound. I remembered it from my childhood. It was the sound we made when we played in the tub. When we'd cup our hands and push them down into the water.

Whuump.

"What the hell was that?" was my first fully conscious thought. And it didn't just bubble up; it was a thought with priority and volume. I might have even said it or mumbled it in dream-speak.

No sound for the moment, but I could sense the presence of whatever it was and it was stopped out in the water. Mentally I triangulated that most peculiar sound to within a few yards off the shore of the lake. I tried to position myself to get a look without making any noise which, at my age, could not be guaranteed. There was almost always a creak, crack, or audible groan when I got up in the morning, especially off a thin air mattress on the ground. If the sound I heard was caused by an animal, it would surely be aware of my presence if I tried to wrestle from the confines of my bag. I couldn't risk chasing it off by moving, so I relaxed and closed my eyes and tried to imagine what it was.

I heard it and it sounded large. Larger than a dog. I had seen no sign of predators on the trail to Big Sand Lake the day before, so it probably wasn't a bear or a wolf.

Whuump.

"Oh, I know that sound!" I thought on the edge of discovery. It was long-legged and must have had a big hand or paw or hoof to make a whuump like that. Maybe a deer or an elk. Or a horse or a moose. Aha! It was a moose! And it was walking along the shore!

Whuump.

I was happy but just for a couple of seconds. I remembered moose were in rut in October. They became big gnarly obnoxious bastards

51

during the rut. They'd attack Volkswagens; my little red tent would get thrown about like a kite in the wind by a bull moose in the rut. But whatever it was seemed to be moving on.

Whuump. Plop. Clip clop. Clip clop.

Off it went from the water into the woods. I looked on my wrist; the time was 10 p.m. and it was 28 degrees and the barometer indicated the weather staying overcast. I had only been asleep a couple of hours since arriving at Big Sand and already been welcomed by a moose. There was a mountain goat to greet me when I crossed into the Selway and a moose to meet me at Big Sand Lake. I enjoyed a smile and went back to sleep.

When I woke up in the morning light, I rolled over onto my belly and up onto my elbows to stretch my lower back and to catch up with my journal. I scooched up over the threshold into the vestibule, set up the stove, and brewed some tea while I wrote about the hike to Big Sand Lake. Mostly, I wrote about navigating in the wild. How things were so much different in a designated wilderness area compared to National Forests and parks. How it changed from hiking to trekking.

The Wilderness Act, signed into law in 1964, created the National Wilderness Preservation System (NWPS) and recognized wilderness as "an area where the earth and its community of life are untrammeled by man, where man himself is a visitor who does not remain". Part of the NWPS was the stipulation that no motors of any kind for any purpose were allowed in designated wilderness areas. No ATVs, no motorcycles, no motorized transport allowed. No bulldozers, tractors, power tools, or chain saws, and so on. Passionate beyond words about the wilderness and its unmatched solitude, I am grateful for the Act. But it changed the way most people navigated when they hiked and this is the reason why...

When a tree fell down in a National Forest, the Forest Service cleared the trail. When they had budget money, the United States Forest Service (USFS) sent crews out to clear deadfall and rocks that fell down on the trail. They used chain saws, of course, and they created nice clear trails for the public to enjoy. Hikers could follow well-maintained and clearly marked trails to most popular destinations.

When a tree fell down in a designated wilderness area, however, it could not be cut with a chain saw. Chains saws and power tools were prohibited by the Wilderness Act. To clear the trail, someone must use an axe or a hand-held crosscut saw to remove the fallen tree. You might be able to hike around; if not, you endure some old-school back-breaking work. Imagine cutting through a Ponderosa pine that fell across the path. It might be 3' thick and take an hour or longer to cut by hand. If it could be moved off the trail after a single cut, you were fortunate. If not, it had to be cut again to clear the trail. Finally finished, you walked on to find another tree a hundred yards ahead. And this happened from one end of the wilderness to the other.

Without a chain saw, hard physical labor with the most rudimentary of tools was the only way to clear miles of trail. Consequently, trail maintenance in the wilderness suffered; if the Forest Service didn't have time or money for the job, trails were only cleared by outfitters or others who worked there. They only cleared them if they had no other choice. Seldom-used trails in the wilderness became overgrown and clogged with deadfall, or faded into a maze of game trails through the forest. It could be unnerving to the uninitiated, but it was part of the backcountry experience. There wasn't always a trail to follow in the wild.

I scratched the beard that began to grow on my face and read through what I had written. I added the part about the moose walking by and then put the journal to the side. I pulled on my clothes, ate breakfast, and cleaned up. I camped on the eastern shore of the lake in between logs on the edge of a marsh. There were lots of reeds and driftwood, and the water was as still as the morning. I decided to check out the perimeter of the lake. I grabbed my sticks and started hopping logs along the shallow shoreline to get across the water and walk around the lake. I followed the tracks by looking through the still water to confirm that my visitor was, in fact, a moose and to learn from whence he came. My boots were great for that kind of play; I felt confident jumping from rock to rock or tree to tree. I made my away around to the main trail again and followed it on down the side of the lake.

Big Sand was roughly oval and a bit less than a half mile long. Almost twenty miles into the backcountry and situated at 5700', the lake was entirely mine to enjoy. The hillside on the northern side of the lake had burned, but new growth was visible and symbolic. Otherwise, Big Sand was pristine. I stepped through the rocks and deadfall as I worked my way along the north shore. The western side was thickly forested and, to my surprise, there was a campsite in the trees. Campers, probably fishermen from the summer, had built a fire ring and there were cleared spots for tents. As was customary, the campers left some kindling and firewood by the ring for the next visitor which happened to be me. I smiled appreciatively. It wasn't human contact, but it was close. I walked through the campsite to finish my reconnaissance of the lake. The forest grew thicker and thicker as I moved through the south part of the lake. One of the feeder creeks came in and the water spread out; in another couple hundred yards, I was back to my campsite in the reeds.

I sat down with some trail mix and creek water, and reviewed my findings while I ate. The north side was rocky and burned, the western edge was lush, the southern side was thick and boggy, and the east side was wet. There were signs of wildlife everywhere and the scenic view was best from the western side which might be the reason they cleared for a camp there.

"Well, there ya' go…" I said out loud and tossed the last of the peanuts and raisins into my mouth. I got up to move my camp and continue my day on the other side of the lake.

Adventure was commonly associated with travel. It need not be; my adventure involved traveling, but the trek was only a vehicle for the real adventure. The real adventure for me was letting go of everything I had defined as important and conducting another experiment with my life. Technically, adventure was defined by Merriam-Webster dictionary as an "exciting or remarkable experience", which implied that the word was comprehensive and included activities other than travel or trekking. Many of my personal adventures involved some aspect of alpinism because I was drawn to the mountains, but another person's adventures may include volcanoes. Or they may be excited by the adventure found in starting a new career. Adventure meant different things to different people. I was not advocating that everyone start trekking, but I did believe that everyone benefitted from introducing some adventure into their lives. It stimulated growth and enriched our lives. All it required was imagination.

I had a wild imagination for adventure. A child's enthusiasm. As a youngster, I wanted to be a great explorer, but I seemed to lack the skills and confidence I felt were prerequisite. At best, I was an average athlete and struggled academically. But my imagination found ways to work around obstacles that blocked my path to adventure. I found ways to talk myself into doing scary but exciting things. I learned how to walk through my fears and into the life I wanted to live. I used my imagination to come up with ideas for adventures, to imagine responses to all the reasons the quests were unrealistic, and to imagine myself braver and more capable than before. I learned through experience that when we imagine in detail an adventure that excites us, research it, and start talking about it, inevitably the idea begins to manifest itself in your life. And the intensity of the adventure you experience will be proportionate to the immensity of your imagining.

I thought about that as I set up camp on the western side of Big Sand Lake. Letting my imagination run loose had opened the door to this adventure; knowing the power of imagination and practicing with it has made all the difference in my life. As it could in anybody's life.

I decided to use the fire ring and set about gathering wood. It was obvious that Big Sand was home to a lot of wildlife. The habitat was in the throes of autumn and the season's colors collected by the camp site. Deadfall for firewood was abundant and never very far, water was only steps away, and the view over the fire pit and across the lake was nothing less than spectacular. Mostly I gathered handfuls of finger-sized kindling; not just a few sticks but ten or twelve handfuls. I went back to pick up larger branches I had noticed while gathering kindling and made a pile the size of a couple of pillows. I looked around the ground for a handful of twigs, grass, and small pieces of bark. I placed the handful of small stuff into the fire pit and lit it with some pitchwood. I tended it for a couple of minutes and added kindling as the flames grew. When the fire stabilized, I piled up branches on it and sat back for the show.

As the last light of day disappeared, an owl hooted a steady rhythm from the thick trees by the south edge of the lake. A striped chipmunk scurried between hiding places and searched for leftovers from my meal. The sun set behind my left shoulder and cast its last light on the mountains that were the backdrop for my evening view. The mountains were framed by trees on the sides and by the lake on the bottom. Alive and eternal, flames danced in the fire pit for me in the Selway-Bitterroot Wilderness.

I had no other plans for the evening; no other programs to view. I imagined that I was making progress in a trek across the Rockies, and that my body was whole and my spirit was strong. I watched the fire grow as darkness fell and savored that manifestation of something imagined. I was less than a week into a seven week trip and only a few weeks away from a much colder and snowier experience, but I felt that I was where I needed to be – mentally and physically – to handle the unavoidable hardships. There was something soothing about Big Sand Lake. Fire night was my second night there and I was certain to stay for a couple more. The time was marked only by night and day; I had overcome the need to plan things. Lying back against an old dead tree, I stared into the black distance behind the dancing flames and settled into comfort with the trek. I had what I needed to complete the adventure and I knew it. There grew a feeling of confidence I had not experienced in a great while. I crossed my legs at the ankles and my arms across my chest and tried to melt into my seat. Across the lake, I could hear a moose whuumping by the water's edge.

The only bad thing was that my brain still buzzed. Thought storms often made it difficult for me to fall asleep and brain lightning flashed until early morning following the night that I moved camp. I had hoped that the time alone and a good fire trance would help me nod off and enjoy a long night's sleep. Unfortunately, my unquiet mind persisted. Instead of fighting, I went with it. If I couldn't sleep, I would do something else until I got sleepy and then sleep until I no longer felt tired. It was simple. Uncomplicated. Obvious.

I got up the next day at 10:30 committed to doing absolutely nothing except eating and resting and writing. I spent the whole day doing each of those things with enthusiasm. The luxury of time allowed me to pick raisins out of my trail mix to add to my breakfast oatmeal. I changed socks and skivvies, washed the dirty ones out in the lake, and gave myself a splash in the process. I wasn't going to bathe in the icy water, but it was invigorating to wash my hair and pits and privates. I trimmed my nails and warmed myself in a clean base layer and fresh skivvies. I let my boots and feet air out. I assembled wood and stone into a primitive chaise lounge and napped for a couple hours in the afternoon. I wasn't on vacation; I was living a new way of life. Whether it lasted months or years or the rest of my days, I only concerned myself with living day-to-day the life I had imagined. In the late afternoon, I laid out my maps to look over where I might go from Big Sand.

With most things planned, I started at the end and worked my way back. That is to say that I started at the destination on a map and found a route by working backwards toward my location. It's the same with planning towards a goal; as the famous promoter Jerry Weintraub said, "Envision the goal, then work your way backwards". I looked for the Lochsa River on the upper left quarter of the topo map and, when I found it, traced it up towards Lolo while I looked for the Powell Ranger Station. The Lochsa River, pronounced 'lock-saw', was about 70 miles long and provided one of the longest continuous stretches of whitewater in the world. The name itself came from the native Nez Perce word for 'rough water'. Its headwaters were near the Powell Ranger Station north of the SBW. Brenda and I had noticed the ranger station was only a few miles from the trail up Wendover Ridge, my gateway to the Lewis & Clark trail. We had agreed to meet by Powell Ranger Station when I needed to reprovision. When I found that target on the map, I worked back to Big Sand from there. I had already decided that, unless I changed my mind, I would travel to Hidden Lake whenever I left Big Sand and I spotted Hidden Lake on the map.

There wasn't much information available on Hidden Lake when I planned the route. It looked to be the largest lake in the northeast corner of the SBW and was within the boundaries set for the trek.

Hidden Lake was only 3 miles north of Big Sand, but the mountain between the two lakes turned it into a nine-mile trip. I counted three creek crossings on the map. The hike started to the west and curled to the north around the mountain between the lakes, then headed east to finish up due north of my departure point. It seemed to always turn to the right so the hike formed the shape of the letter 'C'. I expected it to be of average difficulty, but the map suggested that a lot of elevation gains could make it tougher.

I read the maps for an hour or more. I searched along the intended route, searched for previously unnoticed possibilities for exploring, and I embedded waypoints and natural landmarks into my brain. I looked for Colt Killed Creek, also called White Sand Creek, and followed it to the Lochsa. I looked over the area around Powell Ranger Station and the Lochsa Lodge beside it. I tried to familiarize myself with the logging roads around those two facilities, but there were too many of them and they twisted and turned and intertwined. When I got there, I would bushwhack my way from Colt Killed Creek to Lochsa Lodge or the ranger station.

I traced the blue line marking Colt Killed Creek as it meandered down the map from the ranger station to Hidden Lake and made the 'C' going from Hidden Lake to Big Sand. It was a lot of ground to cover. I folded up my maps and stowed them and made the decision to pack out in the morning. As much as I enjoyed the comfort and beauty of Big Sand Lake, I was on a trek – not a camp out. It was time to start moving again.

Hidden Lake

Breaking camp took a fraction of the time it had taken at the beginning of the trip. I rolled up, stuff-sacked, and packed for the trail in 20 minutes, and that included an extra-large breakfast. I sat on my heels, looked at the sun rise over Big Sand, and enjoyed my last morning there. I finished my tea and stood to load up.

I pulled the pack up against my leg. I dipped quickly to position my right shoulder through the strap when I picked the pack up off the ground. It was like a dance move and I met the pack halfway through the turn. I jammed my left arm through the left shoulder strap as I finished the lift-and-turn and, before the weight set fully on my shoulders, I bent over and cinched the hip belt. An extra shove of the pack upwards before fully tightening the belt kept the load high on my hips. When I straightened up, load balance was tuned using the shoulder straps and load tugs. Lastly, I slid Big Thump into the holster on my chest. There was no stress or strain; any lingering physical signs of the city life were gone. Nothing soft or soggy. I turned my better self up the trail and grinned at the prospects for the day.

For the first couple hours, I had some sun on my back. The air was so clear that objects stood out from their backgrounds. There was a ridgeline to my right that looked less than a mile away; it was surreal because of its clarity. The group of peaks that included Diablo and Hoodoo on my left were colorful and detailed even though they were several miles distant. I stayed to the right as the trail diverged at stream crossings and at random. My wristwatch barometer indicated a rising trend and high pressure usually meant good weather. I hoped to feel some sunshine soon. The weather had been great for so late in the year; there had been only dustings of snow and very little rain. The temperatures were mild during the days and nights. However, it had been cloudy most of the time and I hoped for some warm clear days before the snow moved in for the winter. Judging by the graph displayed on my barometer, the cell would be over us in a day's time. I would have clear skies for a couple days which would warm my days and chill my nights. I looked up from the barometer (which was part of a wristwatch device that also served as an altimeter and thermometer) to survey the sky and sample the wind. By habit, I inhaled deeply through my nose and exhaled sharply, then inhaled another sample more deeply. Switching from digital to analog, I used the tools with which I was born. My eyes analyzed, categorized, and tracked the clouds. My ears and skin calculated wind speed and humidity, and my nose tasted the weather. Like watching a dashboard while driving, I kept my attention on the sky all day as I walked along the trail. In the backcountry, I smelled things before I saw them and that included weather. So, as Jeremiah Johnson was advised, I kept my nose in the wind and my eyes along the skyline.

The sun reached its zenith and the shadows fell behind me. Things moved slower in the afternoon than in the morning, maybe the result of a fading pace or the trail's ups-and-downs. I came around the top of the 'C' and finally saw the other side of the peak that separated Big Sand and Hidden Lake.

The burn from the 2007 fire staggered me; it seemed to have exfoliated the entire drainage. Like black mold overgrowing the hillside, standing bones of a forest stood as a haunting reminder of nature's emotionless fury. Some trees were burned only on one side leaving a streak of gray to contrast the black of burned bark. Their remaining limbs, thicker on the southern side, looked like the burnt limbs of a corpse reaching out to escape the ferocious heat. Hidden Lake was down in that burn and its unsightliness weighed heavy on my heart. The trail split and I veered to the right toward the middle of the drainage to the lake. There was a lot of wildlife sign and that was encouraging; at least the habitat still sustained life. The smaller plants and bushes were healthy. It had been six years since the fire and three foot pine trees grew tenaciously amongst the destruction. It was a natural event and the forest would grow back healthier, but that truth was lost in the sorrow of the Halloween-skeleton forest. I moved slowly and silently as I worked my way to the lake. There was snow on the tops of the mountains that tried to mask the ugly truth, but the burn revealed itself. The day seemed colder and grayer because of it. After walking a mile south into the drainage, I came upon Hidden Lake.

The first impression was ancient burial ground spooky. As though admonishing me for dwelling on the visual, however, the lake put out a tangible vibe.

"Don't be fooled by what you see. Life is bursting from the crust."

I looked down at the ground around my feet. There was dirt and grass and some of the grass was still green. The spindly dried stalks with cotton-ball tips were dry only because it was fall. They were healthy and abundant and turned out to be great fire starters. The fire of 2007 had not sterilized the seeds scattered on the ground, so recovery was underway and evident.

I walked closer to the lake. I stood on its northern edge and looked across to the south. I examined the perimeter closely and searched it for animal life. It appeared a beaver dam to the northeast had created a small pond attached to Hidden Lake and the pond looked like the head on a round snowman's body.

Facing south, I had the best exposure to the sunshine I expected for the next couple days. There were some trees that had escaped the fire on the other side of the lake. I figured the best place to set up camp was right where I stood. I looked for something flat and safe to use as a site for my camp. In burns, it was a bad idea to sleep under a dead tree that was leaning over you and there were a lot of them in that area. But in short order, I had my gear laid out. I rested easily on the ground facing south and looked over my toes at the lake. With my fingers laced behind my head, I stretched out the back that carried the pack all day.

In time, two small flocks of ducks circled into their separate spots on the lake. Neither flock had more than five ducks, but there were bound to be others.

"Don't be fooled by what you see. Life is bursting from the crust."

Yes, there was life at Hidden Lake. But there was a perceptible melancholy, as well. Great swaths of the wilderness were scorched. No amount of new undergrowth could cover the disfigurement of the burn. I tried to be philosophical about it while soaking in its vibe, but it was hard to get past the physical trauma. With the exception of the ducks, a few fish that surfaced, and the bits of undergrowth, Hidden Lake looked as lifeless as the moon.

It warmed enough to unzip my jacket, and I laid back and closed my eyes. The cloud cover broke up and allowed the sun to shine through. Cloud shadows passed over my face followed by light and warmth that felt like an autumn comforter. The wind had begun to die down and I knew that warm weather had arrived. I drifted in and out of sleep stretched out on the ground by Hidden Lake.

I woke to the sound of jet fighters screaming as they streaked by close overhead. I woke up confused, certain that I was mistaken but taken by the unmistakable sound. Maybe I had been dreaming. There was nothing in the sky. No sound left behind, no contrails. I sat up and took some water to rinse around in my mouth. Another drink to clear my throat. Again, the air ripped above me, pushed by something fast, only this time it seemed lighter. Fully awake, I focused on the area surrounding and just above the lake. Above some treetops, I saw a flicker of movement coming down the left side of the lake. It was a flock of bluebill ducks or maybe ring-necks. I had heard they made a jet-like sound when diving into lakes from higher altitudes, but I had no idea it would be so realistic. Even while I watched them and timed the sound to their movement, I was fascinated by the noise they created. They landed and fed for a while, and moved from time to time. They fed at the lake for the rest of the day.

I got up to check things out. I hadn't walked the perimeter since taking off my pack. I moseyed off to the left toward the head of the snowman; I wanted to see the pond and the dam that built it. The ground was easy to move over; not too rocky or too much deadfall. I stayed close to the edge of the lake. There were fish in it; I saw them from the shoreline. There was one or two at a time, spread out by the shore. Not a lot of fish, but clearly life existed in the lake. Ahead I saw where water left the main body of the lake over a natural spillway to feed the pond created by the beaver dam. It grew louder as I approached. It was not particular fast or voluminous, but the spillway was wide enough that it served as a gurgling water slide and created a calm and relaxing ambiance. The pond sat a bit lower than the lake and I looked it over as I listened to the spillway.

I imagined what Hidden Lake might have looked like before the fire. I imagined the trees full of bark and green needles, and the things I might hear but couldn't see because of all the trees. And the forest creatures in the trees.

I imagined but they did not manifest. There may have been life coming from under the crust, but it would take a hundred years to break through. I was not depressed by what I saw at Hidden Lake. I knew that fires were Nature's way of cleaning things up a bit and I saw lots of evidence of a strong comeback. I was sad in a selfish sort of way; sad because I wouldn't be there in a hundred years to see it fresh and new.

However, I was intrigued by the unexpectedly strange vibe at Hidden Lake. It was undeniable. I was not new to high forests or mountains, but the feeling that came over me upon my arrival at Hidden Lake was a new experience. There was pain in the destruction and I was saddened by it.

I slept well enough the first night at Hidden Lake. The evening sequence of events had become routine. A tuna pouch warmed against my stomach inside my clothes and then eaten by the fire, an hour of journaling, and to bed a couple hours after sundown. I got up the next morning and took advantage of the warm sunny day. I washed clothes with bio-degradable soap and scrubbed them on big rocks in the lake, then rinsed them twice and watched as two weeks' worth of funk and filth spread out through the water. I thought how it might poison the fish and they'd turn belly up and float to the surface because of my stinky socks. The thought ignited a laugh that exploded, shot across the lake, and startled every living thing on the surface. I took a bath in the ice cold water. It was shocking at first but so refreshing and invigorating. It was a funny sunny day.

The second night, however, I did not sleep. The thought storms were overwhelming and disturbing in their content. On that night, storms flashed around issues both infuriating and depressing, and I tried to stand against their fury. A dark rider had come to collect me and I fought the urge to join him in anger and depression. He battered me with all manner of torturous thought: bone-breaking hate, gut-wrenching regret, and fantasies of self-justified revenge. The Observer knew that it was only illusion, only a chemical flash fire, but I burned alive in the emotions created by the storm. I struggled to find sleep, but sleep did not come that night.

Physically and emotionally spent, I walked around the lake toward the beaver pond as soon as the sun came up. I sat by the spillway and let it cool my burning brain. I laid down on the rocks and tried to sleep, but could not relax and soon went back to camp for breakfast. The previous night left me empty. I walked around the other side of the lake and, for the first time on the trip, felt alone. Since there wasn't much to see on that side of the lake, I walked back down to the spillway, a more comfortable place to be alone.

I felt the spirit of my daughter, as if she were thinking of me. She had accompanied me on a couple wilderness adventures and had some idea what was happening. She was always tough and traveled well. She brought her own special offering of peace to the forest. None of my kids were big fans of cold camping, but Paloma might have enjoyed the Selway. The scenery and pace and solitude would be a good fit for her.

As I thought of her, a lone white duck circled the pond. I looked up at the duck as if it had called to me and watched as it circled a second time. Then it settled into the water. It did not start to feed upon landing, but instead turned toward me, paddled a few strokes, and quacked. Then it turned away and drifted and fed the rest of the afternoon. I wondered where it came from and Paloma came to mind. I chuckled at the thought that my daughter had come to Hidden Lake as a white duck to check on me. I was glad she came, too. I stood up by the water and did a waltz for her and sang out loud as we danced by the spillway. She filled the hollow spot that burned in me that morning, when loneliness was the feeling of hunger while fasting. She spoke to my soul and I felt better with her company.

I decided to leave Hidden Lake the next morning. No need to stick around; plenty of other places to see. It was a most mysterious place, but I decided it was time to go. As I headed into the tent, I took note of how bright the clear sky was that night. It was going to get cold. I looked across the stars and noticed the source of the great night light.

The moon was full.

"Well, that makes sense," I thought out loud. And then I laughed as I shook my head. I zipped the door closed and drifted off in the extreme isolation of my cocoon.

Freewheeling

I woke up cold on a cloudless morning. There was frost on everything and a hint of ice ringing the rocks on the edge of the lake. The hot tea was so good I had a second cup. I felt the changing of the seasons.

Hidden Lake was part of a 20-square-mile ecosystem that included Hidden Lake, Hidden Creek, Hidden Peak, with Hidden Creek Ridge connecting all those components via east/west ridgelines and spurs. I left the lake for the ridge and used it to travel the rest of the day. But first, I had to cross Hidden Creek and I wasn't thrilled about it. It was easy, nothing dangerous, but I just didn't want to do it.

Hidden Lake was surrounded by steep mountains that blocked out the sunlight in the morning. No sunlight at all, everything was cold, especially the water. I didn't usually care about the temperature; I liked winter trekking. I liked being out in the cold. But it mattered that morning when I arrived to cross Hidden Creek because I had to cross through cold water. The water in the creek was so cold, it would have been ice if not moving so fast. It was big and rapid and too damned cold to cross first thing in the morning. Never having been a person who enjoyed fording rivers and creeks, I grumbled while I removed my gaiters, boots, and socks and strung them around my neck. I squawked when I stepped off into the numbing cold of almost frozen water. And it seemed like small sharp rocks conspired to send me stumbling face-first into the creek under a heavy pack to drown in a few inches of water. Damn bad way to start the day; that's how I felt gearing up on the other side.

My objective for the day was what seemed to be a meadow on the map where Big Flat, Big Sand, and Colt Killed Creeks converged. Rather than scramble down the drainages and through the creek bottoms, I thought it clever to run a shortcut to Hidden Creek Ridge and scramble down a spur directly into the meadow. I needed a stiff workout. I strapped the pack in tight to my sides so it wouldn't roll as I bushwhacked and struck off-trail over an unnamed spur.

First, I ascended a few hundred feet and rounded a knob to the ridgeline. The knob was the first of several false summits on the way to Hidden Peak. Since the ridge was within the tree line, my vision was obscured and landmarks were hidden. Hidden Peak was hidden. I didn't need to see it, but I didn't like losing the advantage of perspective. It did, however, add to the difficulty of the route-finding puzzle. After I followed the ridge for a couple of hours, I looked for the spur on the left that would take me down to the meadow. I wasn't walking through a jungle, but the trees were thick enough to block the big picture. I couldn't see well enough to get my bearings in unfamiliar country, so I sat down and got organized. I wasn't lost, but I didn't know where I was relative to my objective. I got out the GPS device to pinpoint my location.

My bushwhacking efforts took more time than anticipated and I wasn't as far along the ridge as I thought. After identifying a couple landmarks that could be seen above the trees, I took a compass reading on my target. I ate some jerky and drank some water; I was having a wonderful time. Part of the reason I had chosen the Selway-Bitterroot Wilderness was to navigate in the wild and I was navigating the backcountry on that day. It took hours to get to the meadow. Stands of trees opened up into small alpine bogs where standing water would hide in tall grass and create a swamp in the middle of nowhere. Deadfall trees were scattered everywhere; there was no straight-line path to anything. Once I reached the spur I traveled down it and connected crossings thru deadfall and tall grass and water and mud. Some trees couldn't be stepped over; I had to roll over them or go around. I constantly changed direction. When open ground allowed it, I bounded down the slope in long, stretched-out steps. My quadriceps pumped and burned as they managed the grade and changes in tempo. I picked up speed through a maze of deadfall, weaved my way over and under and around, all the while carrying a 50 pound pack. It felt like play, but if I slipped or fell and broke a bone or got gored by a branch, the situation would be most serious. My sticks clicked and my legs pumped, so I let go and rode my body down the hill. It was exhilarating. I came out of the trees and caught sight of a creek on my left about a quarter mile away. I connected with the creek trail at the bottom of the spur and went downstream to the right to find a crossing. I found a place to set camp for the night close enough to the creek to make it easy to get water. I put my air mattress on the ground outside my tent and laid down to rest for a while.

I felt so free, so forgiven of the debt of responsibility. Liberated from the yoke of expectation, I was free to recreate myself and my relationship with the world. I laid on the dirt floor of a massive living room and enjoyed the view to the northwest. I sipped some water, but I wasn't hungry. I wasn't in a hurry. I wasn't bored. Talk about living in the moment; those moments by the confluence at the bottom of the spur were moments that lived forever. I had become more intimate with the wilderness during my stay at Hidden Lake, more emotionally invested. Consequently, I felt more welcome. I felt thoroughly at home.

After a half-hour's rest, I got up and made a protein drink. I took a little walk in search of Colt Killed Creek. Essentially, I had come to a 'Y' in the road; I had to ford Colt Killed Creek and select one of two routes. The route to the right traveled northeast and would take me to White Sand Lake, an optional stay-over that might prove to be fun. Or the route to the left traveled northwest, which would take me to Powell Ranger Station where I had to go to reprovision.

I sipped the orange-flavored shake and pondered my options. It was the 20th of October and I was only halfway to the food drop which meant I had to pick up the pace. I didn't have to hurry but had to keep moving. White Sand Lake was identified in guide books as a secluded destination and it was only six to seven miles up the trail. If I went right to visit White Sand, I would use three days minimum and return the way I came. The trail down Colt Killed Creek would take me into deeper canyons and along more wild and scenic water, and was in the direction I eventually needed to travel. I sipped on my protein and leaned toward going left. I had been doing the secluded lake thing for a couple weeks and heard the call of Colt Killed Creek over a side trip to White Sand. I squatted by the creek, rinsed out my bottle, and refilled it with fresh water.

I took a closer look at the crossing I had planned for the morning. It looked more like a river than a creek. It was wide and fast and there were some deep pools, it seemed. I stared at the dark spots on the bottom under the rushing surface water. I couldn't tell if they were big black moss-covered rocks or deep holes. As it was, I was going to have to strip up to the waist to stay dry. I wasn't looking forward to dropping into a pocket and maybe sinking to my chest in ice cold water wearing a bulky pack. I would certainly remember to unbuckle the pack straps during the crossing; I didn't want the pack weight to drag me down if I slipped under water. I walked along the shore but could find no better crossing. And I complained about crossing Hidden Creek earlier that day! It was a trickle compared to the wide water in front of me. But there was only one way to move forward with the trek and that was to cross the river… or creek… or whatever the hell it was. Then I would spend the next week or ten days following Colt Killed Creek as it grew larger and louder and wilder.

I turned back toward camp and sauntered up the trail in the other direction. The habitat changed. Foliage was thicker and there was more running water. I stopped at a small stream before I stepped through it. It was stunningly picturesque. I spent too much time trying to capture the sight and sound on video, but video was a poor substitute for experiencing that micro-world. The moss lay like plush doilies on the stones, filtered pure water, and produced a primal calm. The stream stretched only a few feet across, but there were no less than seven small waterfalls singing in harmony. Tiny crystal waterfalls spreading even sheets of water no more than a foot in width and tumbling the same distance down. Like a small stand of mushrooms under water, they were whatever color was made by the light passing through the water against a backdrop of deep greens and gray. A perfectly miniaturized world of water and sound that would seem like Heaven to some, a sanctuary in which to rest and heal. I gave up on trying to capture the scene and gave in to its breathtaking beauty. I listened to Nature say her prayers to God.

The wolves howled that night. Clearly, distinctly, and not far away. The serenade did not last long, but it served as an exciting reminder that the trek was about to change again. Colt Killed Creek marked the transition from a long lazy hike through the Selway to a more serious trek on the Lolo. The wolves welcomed me and I went to bed knowing I would soon begin the next stage. I stretched out in my bag to wind down from the exciting day. I wanted to sleep, but I tossed and turned. I sang and recited and fell back on a meditation technique I learned as a hippie. Nothing worked; I had a movie playing in my head and I could not go to sleep. Then I realized the problem; mentally, I was still on the trail.

The day had been so physically and mentally intense that, when I closed my eyes, the trail still flew by under my feet like a simulator. I was swept up in the constant movement. Switchback left, switchback right – I visualized this in my brain even when my eyes were closed. I imagined my knees flexing to take weight off of my back as I traveled downhill. Like a skier, I stayed with the fall line and my poles searched forward for pace and placement; a bit of grace in a brutish undertaking. More focused in the center, my vision blurred on the edges where deadfall would passed by my side like a guardrail and things blurred when I picked up speed. The playback of the day wouldn't stop. It seemed an endless loop of lesson video that my mind studied and filed away. I laid on my back and did relaxation exercises for my body. Somewhere in the night, I fell asleep smiling, tickled by the funny ways my brain was working on the trail.

Colt Killed Creek

While breaking camp and eating breakfast, I remembered I had to cross Colt Killed Creek that morning. It was not a pleasant thought. As I previously mentioned, I was not a big fan of fording waterways. It was not the water; I was a swimmer in high school and a certified PADI Divemaster. It was the hassle associated with the way I trekked: in winter with extra gear, solo so I carried EVERYTHING, and extended stays so there was a lot to carry a long ways alone. No complaints, mind you; that was how I liked it. But it was generally a lot of weight in winter and when I finally got upright and moving forward only to have to stop and remove my boots for a crossing... Well, it was never my favorite part.

Inexplicably, I felt the need to voice my objections. I tried to be respectful of my surroundings, but I needed to object with passion and corresponding volume. If those junk-yard mountain hyenas could express themselves vocally in the middle of the night, I thought it appropriate, even important, that I let Nature know of my presence and general attitude.

"Goddam crossings..." I grumbled, not shouting... more like a dog growls before it barks. A sharp painful stone poked my foot just to annoy me. "You'd think after a million years that the bottom would be worn smooth as a sidewalk, right?"

Not a bird chirped. Ground squirrels dropped their nuts and stood up, eyes and ears forward. The wind died down to listen.

"If hunters came through here regularly, there'd be a pack bridge across this waterway, I can promise you that."

I walked into the roiling water, naked up to my waist, backpack heavy and decorated on the outside with boots and camera and dangling socks. I walked forward cautiously because the stones hurt and sometimes shifted. I was glad for my sticks for keeping me upright. I talked as I forded and all the forest listened intently.

"Good God, I need a ferry to get across this thing!" I bellowed. "I should have waited for low tide. Or maybe this IS low tide!"

My grousing changed to laughter and my spirits lifted as the exit came within sight. I warned myself not to get in a hurry. I negotiated the final few yards to a victorious crossing. After reaching the other side, I dried, got geared up, and turned with the trail to go downstream with Colt Killed Creek.

"Goddam creek. That's a river in Texas!"

Not a bird chirped. Not a wolf within miles.

That day's hike was strong. My legs felt like pistons driving the machine that was my body up and over hill after hill. There wasn't a lot of thinking to do. The terrain changed, so I adjusted. I side-hilled on a steep well-timbered face a few hundred feet above the creek and the top of the ridge above me was out of sight. The hillside on the other side of the creek was a painting of fall colors at their peak, some natural and some not so much. The change in terrain made the trees look taller and the pattern of color changed. There were strokes of color instead of spots; all of the colors one could hope for in a forest. But there was a rusty copper color from trees killed by beetles. The beetle blight infected the Rockies in Idaho and

I saw their presence in the colors on the hill. The trail itself seemed open and easier to navigate, and I covered many miles. I had two more water crossings that day; they could have been easier to negotiate but I didn't want to take my boots off again. I chose to hop across fallen trees, stones, and boulders as opposed to wading through the water. I felt strong and nimble and trusted my instincts. It was a wonderful part of the trek.

The next few days brought me closer to the high point of the trip. The month spent in the SBW was a month of preparation for the Lolo Trail. Soon, I would be able to relate my surroundings and experiences with my heroes, the greatest adventurers in the history of our country. And Colt Killed Creek was my first contact with that part of the trek.

(from the journals of Lewis & Clark - September 14, 1805 (Colt Killed Creek))

> "here we wer compelled to kill a colt for our men & Selves to eat for a want of meat & we named the South fork Colt Killed Creek and this river we call Flathead River [*currently Lochsa River – the author*]. The mountains which we passed to day much worst than yesterday the last excessively bad & thickly strowed with falling timber & Pine Spruc fur hackmatak & Tamerack, steep & stoney our men and horses much fatigued."

It was no easy thing for the Corps of Discovery to kill one of its horses. The horses had literally saved the expedition. Earlier, when Lewis first laid eyes on the Rockies, he knew he would need horses to complete the trip before winter. He raced up Bitterroot Valley looking for native peoples with whom they could trade. In one of the great moments of serendipity in the world's history of exploration, the Shoshone chief they encountered and with whom they hoped to negotiate for horses turned out to be Sacajawea's long lost brother. There was a great welcoming and reunion, and that stroke of luck enabled a successful passage through the mountains for the Corps of Discovery. The men relied on the horses for their very lives and were loath to eat the animals that carried them through the Rockies. But they were starving and had no other option. They named the creek at the headwaters of the Lochsa as a memorial to the sad event.

I walked out of the SBW late in the afternoon. Everything looked the same when I crossed into the Clearwater National Forest. And so it should; it was only a man-made boundary line on a map. It could mean better trail maintenance. It could also mean signs of humanity. I stepped off the edge of civilization three weeks prior and had no human contact in that time. I was in no hurry to reestablish communication. Even though I was officially out of the Selway-Bitterroot Wilderness, I remained immersed in the backcountry and embraced the isolation. It was peaceful, but not necessarily quiet. I talked to myself as I trekked, spoke loudly and with conviction, and sometimes sang on the trail. Truthfully, it was one of the things I noticed but did not anticipate; the sudden and spontaneous release of emotions. A vocal mind.

Earlier on the trek while I practiced letting thoughts slip by, I learned how to take my time with thoughts of substance. I tried earlier to convey how I had the luxury of using the day to roll things over for better consideration. What began to happen on the trail along Colt Killed Creek was unexpected. I realized the by-product of 'better consideration'. Thoughts considered from new perspectives sometimes led to new conclusions. With some, there was an emotional component. Sometimes it came out as a single lost verse to a song or a funny family scene or just a look on one of my children's faces that I will remember forevermore. But something different happened that day as I crossed into the Clearwater National Forest and it was a thing I knew that I must share with my kids. I recorded the event and a message to my children as soon as I found a place to camp.

(from my personal journal – October 24, 2013)

"Kids; this part is for you.

In about 1973, when I was in high school, one of the most popular entertainers in the world was Leon Russell. He wrote a song that made him famous and was covered by famous artists for the next several decades. It was his masterpiece. Today on the trail, it came out of me as easily as the breath coming out of my mouth and I remembered every word. Every single word. I didn't know I knew the song.

It's strange because I never put this song and your mother together before. Listening to it now in the quiet of my mind, I guess the song does that on its own. I share it with you kids not as a bluesy thing, but as a reminder of a beautiful thing... our love was pure and wonderful, and you children were its gift. And it literally came out of nowhere today. Check it out."

..and I wrote the lyrics of the song for them in my journal.

When I finished, I sat the journal down, leaned forward with my elbows on my knees, and stared at nothing on the ground. No thoughts bubbled up in my mind or any thoughtful considerations, not really any feelings of any kind. There was a sense of emptiness and it expanded throughout my system. A tear fell from my eye. I was surprised and looked down at it. Then another, and another, and unexpectedly I wept. Not a sobbing body wracked by the physical-manifestation-of-heartache weeping, rather a silent emotional waterfall that deepened the creases in my face, eroded any last trace of youth or innocence. I vomited the memories of losing my wife, of losing the family that was my life, of the cost of being 'successful'. I sat in a cold sweat and felt the burning cleanse my hollow core and then felt it subside. It passed leaving only cold sweat dripping from my forehead and the trance-like peace that follows emotional clean-ups. There were no after-affects. With some bad dreams, the funk can weigh a person down for hours even though it's an imaginary event. When my emotional purging passed, it passed. I could have held on to it for a while longer, but I was happy to let it go.

I settled in an outfitter's campground. Since the campground was in a national forest, it did not have the restrictions that accompanied a person in a designated wilderness area. There was a pack bridge across Colt Killed Creek to a rough campground, a large fire ring in the open, and an outhouse on the edge of the camping area. It was clean and well-kept by outfitters who were generally good stewards of the backcountry. The fire ring beckoned to me, so I gathered wood for a fire. The moon was on the backside of its cycle and the sky would be getting darker which would be great for starwatching. Because it was an outfitter's campground, all the close wood had been scavenged, so I searched the creek for driftwood.

I gathered kindling everywhere I encountered it. I loved building fires. As my father used to tell me, "Just like cooking Chinese food; it's all in the preparation." It took some time to haul back several loads and accumulated plenty of firewood for my stay. It was getting colder and colder with every passing day. It was still clear to partly cloudy, but winter was pushing autumn out of the way. I thought about the days ahead and how I probably would not have big fires in the high country. As a result, I decided on building a big bonfire and dancing for the spirits that night. Sort of a goodbye to the Selway.

I stacked the bonfire like a multi-story house. Since I planned on using a lot of wood, it needed a lot of air. I left plenty of room between each layer of logs. In the center at the bottom, however, was the same sized handful of kindling that I use with the same kind of pitchwood. I gathered more big logs for the bonfire. My oldest son, Montana, came to mind. He was a musician. He delivered and recorded live performances of hip-hop, rap, and all kinds of crazy music. We didn't always see eye-to-eye, but we remained heart-to-heart. I acted on the thought of my son in my head and obviously the emotion in my heart, and wrote a song I could perform there at the bonfire in the freestyle manner in which he performed. Of course, the content would be different than his topics of choice, but he would have laughed out loud at my effort. I had a blast looking for the right club with which to keep the beat. I lit the pitchwood and put pitchwood to kindling, and I had some tuna while the fire climbed. When it reached the top of the driftwood tower, I sat on a stump by the fire ring, pounded a steady beat with a stick, and free-styled a song about mountain men for my son wherever he was at the time. A mountain man rap. If it made Montana laugh out loud, I would be most grateful.

Even though they were far away in Texas, I felt my kids with me. As I turned my awareness to them, inhaled their smell from their hair, heard their voices in my mind, I knew what it meant to reach across space and time.

"You're still growing," I thought. A smile so subtle as not to be seen slipped across my face.

It was a raging bonfire, the kind that hypnotized Mankind for untold millennia. Flames were the universal hallucinogen, transfixing every human observer for hours until nothing remains but coals. That bonfire burned until late in the night; the spirits must have been happy.

I fell asleep early and slept until morning. I was comfortable in the outfitter's camp across Colt Killed Creek from the trail. I was well-situated in a place that had good shelter, easy water, and flat comfortable ground; not to mention the outhouse. It looked so out of place. I had moved at a brisk pace since leaving Hidden Lake, so I decided to hang around for another day and relax. And about a minute after making that decision, I was back asleep in my cocoon.

I slept off-and-on until the next morning. I awoke early in the day feeling refreshed and ready to head off towards the Lolo Trail. The morning was cold; not crisp or brisk, but cold. Daytime temperatures were in the low 30s and nighttime temperatures were down in the teens. Ice formed on the edges of things and the hibernators were, for the most part, hunkering down. Condensation was heavy in my tent and my departure would be delayed until the sun came out to dry it. Winter was coming, but I was prepared. I could not have planned any better. Depending on where I made camp, I would signal Brenda in two or three days and meet her at the lodge by the ranger station to resupply for Lolo Trail.

For days, I walked through the Idaho wilderness along the edge of Colt Killed Creek. I shifted my mental focus from where I was to where I was going. I thought about ridge-running on the Lolo Trail. Instead of following creeks around the feet of giants, I would spend my days walking across their shoulders. The weather would become a critical consideration in daily decision-making. The snow would get deep and the work would get hard. The risk factor would increase dramatically. Subconsciously, I increased my pace to get there faster. I couldn't wait to get started on the hard part.

But I didn't want to hurry as I walked away from the Selway. On the contrary, I wanted to savor it. I wanted to collect the colors from the hillsides and the smell of autumn in the air. The sound of water moving at my side was the ambient sound of my days on that trek. In a few weeks, moving water would be hard to find. Some creeks would start icing over soon and I would have to melt snow for water. I would trade the soft and reassuring sound of the creek for the stark clarity of a ridge in the winter. The last few days on Colt Killed

Creek were spent appreciating the scenery and building momentum toward the crux of the trek.

The creek grew larger and faster as I moved further on. The surrounding mountains made their water contributions to Colt Killed Creek as it rushed to become the headwater of the Lochsa. The waterway grew more swollen with every passing mile. The hillsides rose ever steeper, until they appeared too steep to hold soil. A rock kicked off the trail rolled and tumbled until out of sight. I worked the trail hard, striding through the gravel and grass with intent. I was immersed in the trek; I barely felt the pack on my back or the boots on my feet. I saw only color and shape, and heard only the breeze as it shuffled through the leaves, and forgot about food or drink. It was as if I stretched a single happy moment all throughout the day. The creek called to me as it ran downstream looking to connect with a river. It called me to chase, to follow, to catch up. I was hypnotized. Spellbound. Driving a lucid dream.

Finally, when I had no other choice, I stopped. It was twilight and I needed to set up camp. I had side-hilled for miles; there was nothing flat enough to use for a campsite. I walked a little further until I crossed a small stream on the hillside. I grinned a little boy grin as the solution to my campsite problem became clear.

"Sleep out under the stars, strider. That's what Jeremiah would do. Just lay yourself on the uphill side of one of those trees and enjoy the Great Magnificent." I laughed out loud.

The little me inside my head was thrilled with the idea. I scanned the uphill side of trees looking for something sort of flat. I looked up at the sky. It was overcast, but it didn't look like rain. I found a spot behind a large spruce that was flat for about three feet. The tree stood on a small knob, which provided a partial view of the southern sky. I would not be able to see the Big Dipper, but I could sleep out under most of the stars in Idaho and that sounded like fun to me. I dropped my pack but left the tent and sleeping bag inside. I propped it up with wood and rock to level out my sleeping area. I had a full base layer on underneath my trekking pants and a sweater. I pulled my down jacket and Gore-Tex from my pack and began to layer up. It was 4:30 p.m. and the sun dropped fast, so I hustled back to the stream to fill my water bottle and wash my face. I laid my air mattress on the ground on the uphill side of the tree so that it would block me from rolling downhill, and set Big Thump on a rock close by. I fidgeted around a bit to find a good fit and was able to lay on my right side curled around the tree. I used a food sack to prop my head up and watched the stars come out, slowly at first and then brilliantly filling the sky. I was so happy, so pleased to be outside, so close to being one with the world. I don't know when I went to sleep that night out under the stars, but I dreamed with a smile on my face and genuine contentment in my heart.

It got cold that night as the sky cleared. I woke up a couple of times and I thought about breaking out my sleeping bag. But I just ignored my thinking, knowing that cold weather would be a constant companion for the next few weeks. I was uncomfortable but not seriously cold. I opened one eye to look at the sky and the stars were twinkling brightly.

"Bright sky, cold night," I reminded myself. I snuggled up, a man alone in the mountains.

All the while, the creek tumbled and its sound served to relax me. It was better that I didn't sleep that night away, really; one doesn't have too many nights like that in one's life.

I sat up at sun up and I stretched while I walked back to fill my Reactor from the stream. I cooked my oatmeal and drank my tea while I appreciated the night before. I stripped off the Gore-Tex and the jacket and stuffed them in the pack. I filled the baggie in my pocket with trail mix from the Ziploc and brushed my teeth before I headed down the trail.

For two more days, I walked along Colt Killed Creek. I bushwhacked my way to the edge of the creek and spent a cramped night on its rocky shore. I ate oatmeal, jerky, and tuna fish. I lost weight and hardened up. Part of me had changed; I was not the same man that left the truck in Hamilton. Time had changed for me, too. My sticks clicked to a faster rhythm and I traveled many miles in silence.

I had less than six miles to Powell Ranger Station when I sent a signal to my cousin Brenda. We had agreed to use the Self-Test function on my PLB as a digital smoke signal. I sent three Self-Tests which would notify her via email that three tests had been performed five minutes apart. This three-test signal notified my cousin of my imminent arrival at Lochsa Lodge next to the ranger station and signaled her to meet me with provisions to replenish my food supply. I sent the signal as per our agreement and kicked into overdrive. As I neared the coordinates for the ranger station, I came across a number of logging roads. They were unmarked and unruly, curling around blind corners and confusing me terribly. I looked at my map, looked at my GPS device, and looked at the road; none of them matched. I walked a mile or two until the road ended unexpectedly, then I backtracked and tried another route. Finally, I found my way onto a dirt road that seemed to lead somewhere. In the early afternoon, much to my surprise, I popped out of the backcountry on to Idaho Highway 12.

Highway 12 was the only highway that bisected the upper and lower portions of Idaho and it tended to follow the Lochsa River. I had to cross it to get from the SBW to the Lolo Trail. It was the ideal meeting place for a midpoint break in my trek. Our predetermined meeting place was The Lochsa Lodge on Highway 12, but I didn't know if it was to the right or to the left of where I'd come out. I stood on the side of the road contemplating my choices, unaware of my unkempt appearance and unsure why passersby were staring at me. In true mountain man fashion, I made a guess and decided to go left. I made a mental note of my mileage and hoped I was walking the last few miles of the day.

Three miles later, I spotted signage for Lochsa Lodge. I had begun to think I had chosen the wrong direction, but there was the sign and the road to the lodge. Lochsa Lodge was both rustic and comfortable, and was a paradise in this remote part of the country. It catered to hunters, white-water enthusiasts, cyclists, and locals. The dirt road meandered through several cabins that seemed to blend in with the environment and widened as I approached the main lodge, a medium-sized structure of traditional design. There was a large gravel parking lot and a grassy area to the left as I neared the lodge. I noticed a pair of gas pumps and a convenience store across the parking lot from the lodge, and a flat green grassy area behind the store. There was a newer building on the edge of the parking lot. A young man addressed me as I stopped in the parking lot and stared at the mystery building.

"Can I help you with something?"

"What is that?" I mumbled while pointing at the new addition.

"That's the shower and bathroom building. You need a cabin?"

"Yes, sir. Not for me, but for my cousin. She'll be here tomorrow."

"But you don't need one?"

"No, I'm camping out."

"Yeah," he said, smiling. "Should have guessed that."

I had given no thought to my appearance or the questions it might invoke in a stranger's mind. It had been about a month since I last spoken with anyone and I'd been sleeping on the ground the whole time. Other than Hidden Creek, I hadn't bathed. I realized I might look a little rough.

"That a drill motor you got strapped to your chest?" he asked, pointing at Big Thump.

"Huh? Uh, no. No, it's bear medicine. Model 500 .50 Mag. Sorry, I'll stash it in my pack."

"Ain't no one here worried 'bout that. Sure you don't want a cabin?"

"No, thanks. Gotta stay hard. Got a long way to go. But a hot shower sounds pretty good right now. Can I camp somewhere and buy a shower?"

"Sure," he said. "My name is Shad."

I reached out for his extended hand.

"My name is Taylor. Pat Taylor."

"Well, Pat Taylor, you can set your tent up on that green behind the store. No charge for that. The shower will cost you five dollars. I got towels inside the store."

"Outstanding, Shad. I'm going to pitch my tent and I'll be back for those towels shortly."

I scampered over to the green and had camp pitched in minutes. I looked through my pack for something to wear after showering, but my meager pack-out did not include leisure wear or pajamas. I walked around the facility looking for a laundry room. I asked one of the housekeepers for help and she informed me that the lodge had no laundry room for guests. She wasn't actually mean but it felt like it at the time. She was subordinate and didn't want to let me in to the house laundry without her boss's approval. But I'd been on the trail a month and really wanted to clean my clothes. I would wash and dry them myself, no problem. But she wouldn't budge.

I went to the restaurant, ordered a burger, and I chatted up the waitress while waiting for a root beer. Having been almost a month in the backcountry, I conversed with almost every worker who walked by while I gobbled down hot meat and bread. My mouth came alive and my belly expanded to meet the juicy challenge. The beef lifted my spirits and I figured someone would take pity on a dirty old man and let him clean up a bit. By the time I finished my meal, the lady running the gift shop said she would get me some time in the laundry room. Less than an hour later, I was standing in a towel while my clean clothes were drying in the dryer. After folding the last item, I grabbed underwear, my trekking pants, and my sweater and headed to the showers. The physical sensation was indescribable. I made a lot of noise in that stall. It was breathtaking. Of all things luxurious that I had sampled in this world, the hot shower at Lochsa Lodge remained near the top of the list. I milked every drop of hot water from the furnace and blasted every inch of my skin with water almost too hot to touch.

"Oooooh, My God, that's good!" Moans of ecstasy floated out the windows with the steam. To hell with passers-by, I thought; let them laugh.

I washed my hair, rinsed and repeated. I washed my body, rinsed and repeated. My face. My parts. My gnarly hard feet. When the hot water was used, I wiped myself down with soft cotton towels. My skivvies were still warm from the dryer when I slipped my feet through the leg holes. My sweater felt as good as it smelled. I combed my hair, cleaned up the bathroom, and stepped out into the evening air. I had forgotten how good a hot shower could feel.

I went back to the laundry room and took my clean clothes to the tent. I walked over to the convenience store. I bought two packets of peanuts and two Fat Tire beers. It felt as though I was cheating. My clothes and my body were clean, I had a warm meal in my belly and was on my way to two cold beers. But I was on my way to my tent; in spite of the proximity of people with whom I could socialize, I didn't really want to be there. I needed to meet with my cousin and I was happy for the shower, but I was not through being alone.

I woke up in the morning and went outside to pee. Halfway through, still half asleep, I realized that I was peeing on the green grass outside the gas pumps. I quickly looked around; there might have been someone inside the restaurant, but no one outside could see me. I hurriedly slipped back into my tent and got dressed to go eat breakfast.

I walked into the restaurant and was greeted by a pleasant lady who showed me to a table by the fireplace. The big windows on the back looked out past golden tamarack to the snow-capped mountains to the south. The sun was shining through the clouds scattered in the sky. A big man was holding court as he drank coffee and entertained. His voice was as big as his body and his smile could fill up a room.

"Good mornin' to ya'. Hadn't seen you around here before."

"No, sir. I just got in yesterday."

"You the one sleepin' out by the store. Where you from?"

"Selway," I said as I bent down to sip hot coffee.

"Selway? That's a river; not a town."

"Sorry. I meant to say Selway-Bitterroot. I got dropped in near Hamilton, Montana. Walked here from there."

I hadn't caught his name, but he would be easy to remember. He was about 6'7" and probably a former college football player. Maybe in his 50s.

"You walked here from Hamilton? Through the wilderness?"

"Have been for most of the month. Walked over Blodgett Pass, northwest through the Selway up through Big Sand to Colt Killed Creek."

"Are you shittin' me? Abby, go get Gabe. Tell him to get in here."

The waitress went to fetch Gabe the kitchen hand. The big guy kept his eyes on me as he drank from his coffee mug.

"You walked from Hamilton to here last month?"

"Yes, sir. Leavin' tomorrow to finish up Lolo."

"Lolo? In November?"

"Yes, sir. Goin' up Wendover and sortin' it out from there."

Gabe arrived from the kitchen looked suitably disheveled for a 20-something outdoorsman.

"Weren't you tellin' me 'bout spendin' a couple weeks in that Selway-Bitterroot Wilderness area?"

"Yes, sir. Just me and my friend." Gabe sounded rightfully proud.

The big man laughed, then took a big pull on his coffee. Good naturedly, he teased the boy.

"Well, you might get some pointers from this ol' man over here. He spent twice that much time and went it alone!" He laughed large and held his cup out for a refill. "Hell, he looks to be about three times your age, Gabe."

His name was Mitch and he checked my story out with a couple of questions. Though he teased me hard for a stranger, he seemed genuinely interested in the effort.

90

"Hey, Mitch," I redirected during a pause, "what day is it today? I mean, what day of the week?"

He looked at me straight-faced and saw I was serious. He burst out in a bigger-than-life laugh, got up and palmed my meal ticket, and said "Sunday!" He pointed down the hall. "They'll be showing football games on the TV in the bar today. You watched any football this year?"

The blank look on my face answered his question.

"Almost November and you hadn't seen a game…"

He was shaking his head and as he paid the cashier for my breakfast.

"You take it easy, Pat Taylor. I'll see you again sometime."

"Thanks for breakfast, Mitch."

He waved as he walked to his Highway Department vehicle.

I took a late morning nap while I waited for Brenda to arrive. The lodge wasn't very busy; there were some hunters occupying a few cabins, but there were plenty of rooms available and plenty of tables open at dinner. The sun was out and a light breeze danced through the open tent flap. It occurred to me that I had enjoyed spectacular weather during my month in the wilderness. There were some overcast skies and occasional rain, but there were a lot of bright blue skies. I really got lucky when it came to weather in the Selway-Bitterroot Wilderness.

And that late afternoon, as if on cue, the wind tore down through the trees with a vengeance. Within minutes, it was gusting to 40 miles per hour and pellets of sleet were clicking on my tent. Then I heard something I had never heard before in the wild. It was something living being stretched too far. It screeched as it bent to the point of breaking, and the thunderous crack captured my complete attention.

I was full erect and on alert as the rending of fiber gave way to the tree snapping in the wind like a bone made of noise. Every sense strained. The tree reached out to tear at others on its way to early death. I had never heard anything like it, nor will I forget it as long as I live. From a lovely month of autumn to a shearing windstorm spitting hail; it was eerie how the weather changed so dramatically the day after I reached the lodge.

"Bring it on," I said to myself, with the appropriate amount of caution. "I've toted those snowshoes around for a month and I'm about ready to use them."

Brenda arrived with everything and more; all the provisions for the next stage of the trek plus some honey, our laptops so I could download pictures taken in the Selway, and a portable gas stove so she could cook a couple meals. I got her set up in a cute little cabin and she laid out a kitchen on the table. The night that Brenda arrived to the lodge, we had elk steak and salad. Oh, my God! And venison, too. What a delicious treat after a month of oatmeal and jerky. She was excited. We shared lots of stories, she brought lots of reports, and we talked about the trail ahead.

During the time that Brenda and I spent at Lochsa Lodge, I tweaked my load. I removed many items that proved a luxury or unnecessary: a Damascus shawl, extra gloves, ten extra 440 grain rounds for Big Thump, 100 slingshot loads, and a book from which I needed only 7 pages. I also tweaked my diet. I decreased the jerky and increased the trail mix, and added chocolate to the trail mix. This provided more carbohydrates, as did Brenda's homemade dehydrated potato soup, the final addition to the food bag. The bottom line: I reduced my pack weight by approximately 12 lbs. All packed it weighed in at 48 pounds. I was reprovisioned, refueled, and refreshed. We sat around and talked for a couple hours after dinner, then I went to my tent for the night.

Up early in the morning, I fueled up with a big breakfast. Brenda drove me down Highway 12 four miles to the trailhead at Wendover Ridge. It was a 7-8 mile grinding climb that would take me to the top of the first hogback where the real ridge-running began. As we pulled off the road, it was raining. The thermometer in the van read 24 degrees Fahrenheit and the forecast was for more precipitation. I was only slightly on edge. In the final analysis, I had to be tough and in-the-moment to survive the Lewis & Clark trail in winter and I was as prepared as I could be. Brenda jumped out for a hug and a couple of pictures, and drove off leaving me in nasty weather alone eight miles below Wendover Ridge.

Wendover Ridge

Wendover Ridge was probably the most physically demanding section of the Lolo Trail. It was so long and steep that the Corps of Discovery's horses stumbled and fell off the narrow trail. A well-known story told of a horse that fell and rolled down the mountainside for 40-50 yards until it smashed into a tree, destroying Captain Clark's desk in the process.

(from the journals of Lewis & Clark - September 15, 1805 (Wendover Ridge))

> "Steeps assents... party fatigued & horses, several horses sliped and roled down steep hills which hurt them verry much. The one which carried my desk & small trunk turned over & roled down a mountain ... broke the desk the horse escaped and appeared but little hurt... we melted the snow to drink and cook our horse flesh."

It was suitably miserable on the day I began following in the footsteps of Lewis & Clark. I dealt with rain, frozen rain, and fog that drifted through the trees. As I climbed up toward the ridge, the wind increased and the rain was driven into the ground. As the temperature dropped, the rain began to freeze and the hard wind drove the ice pellets stinging into the skin on my face. Big weather rolled in from the northwest and the surrounding mountains were hidden in the clouds. I smelled the changing climate and I sucked the cold into my lungs. Step over step, I hiked up the trail. Mile after mile, the trail climbed the mountain. I stopped at a switchback to put on my shell. It had turned into a Gore-Tex kind of day. Looking out from under my eyebrows, I smirked at the weather and welcomed its threatening presence. I stopped at an overlook for lunch and some tea.

The clouds were stacking up in the sky. The wind grew strong and there was moisture in the air; rain, sleet, or sometimes snow, the sky was falling down. I boiled some water and had a cup of potato soup which I ate as I stood and looked around. The view was different in the Clearwater; it was more densely forested and the ridges seemed to be packed tightly together. Looking off the hillside, I could see ridge after ridge run like lines parallel with the horizon. They were different greenish hues up close, but faded into shades of blue and white until they merged with the clouds in the sky. My instincts told me to enjoy the view while I could, and I soaked in the scenery while I drank my tea.

"Just what I've been waiting for," I remarked as the wind blew stiff and cutting. For me, there was no more awesome feeling than big weather in the mountains. It was raw, without prejudice, and majestic.

I climbed the entire day up to Wendover Ridge. The higher I got, the colder and wetter it got, and the wet rain turned into snow. The high winds had littered the side hill with deadfall and the trail was blocked several times. There was an inch or two of snow on top of rocks and fallen logs. Snow accumulated on the ground too fresh for tracks of man or beast and it covered much of the trail. On one exposed section of the hike, I picked an exit point on the other side of a knob because the trail was lost in the deadfall. I played hopscotch on a windblown patch of ground. Dead trees stood, leaned, or laid like pickup-sticks. I followed the trail as it worked through the deadfall like a fish working through a reef. Sometimes I hopped up and over or sometimes I went around, but I followed the faded trail doggedly for almost a quarter of a mile. All the while, I looked up at where the trail would meet the woods. I couldn't see the exit, but I knew it was there. I had trained for a month in the Selway and felt ready for the test. I let go of the trail and found the best path to the exit. It was like taking off my training wheels. Wendover Ridge made me sweat on a freezing day and took a strict inventory of my skills. It was an appropriate if difficult beginning to the trek on Lolo Trail.

As the day wound down, I looked for a pocket in which to sleep. I stood on a shoulder just below the ridge and found a spot that could be cleared for slumber. It was a quick camp; I needed only to eat and sleep. I looked around for running water; I hadn't seen much during the climb. I found a puddle that, when filtered, would yield the water I needed for a day. After dinner, I slid into my sleeping bag. I rolled over onto my stomach, turned on my headlamp, and laid out my maps.

"Okay… Wendover Ridge finished early tomorrow and Cayuse Junction by mid-afternoon."

I traced the route and visually measured each leg of the day's trip on the map. My body throbbed from the workout. I was completely spent from the long day's uphill effort. It was, indeed, a grueling climb. I was tired but needed to review the next day's route. I woke later in the night with my face in the map momentarily disoriented, then I turned my headlamp off. I rolled over on my side and went back to sleep.

I woke early and easily the next morning. No soreness or body fatigue. I felt the urge to move, to finish Wendover Ridge. To make quick time to Cayuse Junction in preparation for the highest point on the trail.

I held my snowshoes in my hand knowing they would soon be off my pack and on the ground. They featured the latest platform technology. Instead of rawhide lacing over a five foot frame, the new model provided all the flotation a big man needed and were only 9" wide x 30" long. The snowshoes weighed 2.8 pounds and were rated for a 250 pound load. It was a tough purchase to make; I weighed 210 pounds at the beginning of the trip and carried a 60 pound pack (far exceeding the load rating). But I determined that I would be under 200 pounds by the time I needed the snowshoes and that my pack would weigh less than 50 pounds. I pushed the limits of this new technology, but the backcountry snowshoe was shorter, lighter, and easier to pack than the traditional rawhide-laced Alaskan snowshoe. Technology was historically a friend of mine, so I took a chance on the high-tech 'shoes. I looked at the black 5/8" tubing shaped into an oval with one end pulled into a point. Half-inch plastic hangers attached the frame to a gray synthetic decking that provided the flotation. A simple and quick binder held my boots in place and a toothed aluminum claw on the bottom gripped the trail below the 'shoe. At 2.5 feet long and less than a pound and a half each, the snowshoes in my hand seemed too small for the load.

"Better than nothing," I thought out loud. "They'll be fine."

I strapped the snowshoes on the outside of the pack and made ready for the day. It was about nine miles to Cayuse Junction. Even though it was mostly uphill in less-than-ideal conditions, it could be reached in a day. The wind had died down, but the sky was full of clouds and the clouds were full of rain. With temperatures in the low 20s, the rain would be frozen by the time it arrived. I took long steps with pauses at the bottom to stretch out my hamstrings and my hips. I flexed inside my pack frame and moved my weight around to get my balance. I flicked my sticks, pulled my cap down over my ears, and put my boots on the trail.

When I started up the Lewis & Clark trail, the weather was not unlike that described by Captain Clark in his journal.

> "..overcast with low clouds drifting through the pines. Wet & cold."

I started out for Cayuse Junction with the same kind of weather and it got progressively worse. Still more climbing and lots more deadfall to negotiate. And steep. As I gained elevation, the sky got darker and the rain turned to sleet that tic-tacked against my jacket. There is a certain spooky factor that comes into play when thick gray clouds obscure the surrounding mountains and the wind drowns out every other sound. Except the tic-tack of sleet as it smacked against my jacket.

"Persevere," I breathed. I moved with purpose and stood erect against the elements. I would not allow the weather to impose its mood on me. It made me alive.

There was an easiness in my pace that had been absent on the day before; I enjoyed the scene. I started to acclimate, in every sense. I could not linger, however; the climb ate up my time and I was high enough for the frozen rain to turn into fat wet snowflakes. Snow was a magically beautiful thing, but it complicated life on the trail. Less-traveled trails, like the Lolo Trail, were challenging enough. They were not always obvious and could be difficult to find. Snow filled in the trail and introduced a level of uncertainty to the pathfinding effort. To make matters worse, GPS devices did not function well when cloud cover attenuated satellite reception. None of these factors bothered me much, however, as I was on an adventure and uncertainty was my companion. I was good with that and it showed in my laidback gait.

It took an hour to get through the last mile uphill. Fierce wind, steep grade, and lots of obstacles were met with a bit of study and steady resolve. Then suddenly, the trail popped out onto the motorway. I was surprised. It was such a sudden change. A ranger had described it as a one-lane road built back in the '30s by CCC to allow cars to tour along the Lolo Trail. He said it was like an ATV road. Reading the disappointment on my face, he said, "It only overlaps the trail in a couple of places and it can be a lifesaver. Especially if the snow gets deep." After all the struggle getting up to Wendover Ridge, I found myself in the midst of big, soft snowflakes as they drifted down through evergreens framing a track made for a hiker like me. Even with a heavy pack, I stretched out to almost 3 mph on the Lolo Motorway. I made good time toward Cayuse Junction.

A few miles later, I reached the junction and, instead of taking the west fork, I went north. I had read somewhere that ½ mile up the north fork was a small meadow and a creek (I needed water). I traveled 0.64 miles up the north fork and found a little piece of Heaven. I was happy for the good campsite given the wet and cold conditions.

It was a nice flat spot sheltered by frosted firs and carpeted with thick pine needle bedding only a few yards from Cayuse Creek. Despite their name, evergreen needles did not stay green forever. Older needles discolored and dropped off after one or more years, depending on the species. Sometimes the drop occurred slowly; other times, large numbers of needles yellowed simultaneously in late summer or early fall, and made a striking spectacle. The needles formed a thick bed close to good water and it was too nice a site to pass up.

I slid my pack off my shoulders and rested before I set about making camp. I sat on the carpet of yellow needles beneath two evergreen sentries. Under their boughs, I saw Cayuse Creek. Snow clung to rocks and trees, and halos of ice could be found on rocks protruding from the water. And only in eddies; it was not cold enough for moving water to freeze.

I felt the weight of winter as soon as I had begun the climb up Wendover Ridge. There had been more rain and snow during the first two days of the Lewis & Clark trek than the entire trip through the Selway. It was a tangible change in mood. There was no anxiety, but I refocused on the reality of ridge-running in Idaho in November. I had studied the conditions; I was well-versed in winter trekking and prepared for the Lolo Trail, but there arrived that moment when the effort required became a sobering reality. I sat under the trees with my arms circled around my knees. Being prepared for a thing does not make it easy; the next few weeks would be hard. I drank some protein and put my tuna pouch next to my belly. It was going to be an early night.

When I woke the next morning, two inches of icy snow greeted me. It was cold; damned cold. I grabbed the barometer from where it hung above the tent and dove back into my sleeping bag. The temperature read 15 degrees. The gear stashed in the vestibule was literally frozen solid. The damp base layer I removed before crawling into my bag the night before was as stiff as a sheet of plywood. The snow was light and intermittent, but the wind blew strong. I heard it coming out of the north and it sounded like an avalanche. A roller coaster; the wind sounded like a carnival ride building up speed and then hurtling down the steep slope and BOOM! I almost felt it before it arrived. Trees rattled and my tent flapped like a flag in a storm. Mother Nature made sure that everyone knew who was the boss. I was having a full-blown Lewis & Clark experience and it was every bit as fun as that rollercoaster. The wind howled off in the distance, a stark contrast to the flickering white crystals that quietly settled down in front of my tent. I pulled my frozen long johns into the tent and laid them between my ground pads. I hoped they would thaw and dry out; they were of no use to me frozen. I got cozy in my bag, closed my eyes, and listened to the wind. It wasn't long before I was deep asleep.

I slept off and on throughout the day. The weather couldn't seem to make up its mind; the wind and the snow came and went sporadically. The temperature stayed in the teens all day. I walked up and down the creek, a half mile in both directions. I explored Cayuse Junction and discovered nothing worth noting. I passed time until the sun went down. I went to sleep, woke up at 10:20 p.m. and made the following journal entry:

(from my personal journal – November 3, 2015)

> "Can't sleep. I can still hear the snow falling; slowly, but steadily. The next objective (the Indian Post Office) is the highest point on the trail and probably the deepest snow. If I sit here waiting and it doesn't let up, it will make for more difficulties. That plus the bitter cold (my butane lighters won't fire. The thermometer reads 9 degrees) has me considering an alpine start."

On big or technically demanding climbs, one often started out early to allow enough time to get to the top and back. It was called an alpine start. My next camp was many miles away and would require some climbing, and the snow storm would slow me down, so I woke early in the morning to get an alpine start. I got up at 3 a.m. and there were 6 inches of new snow on the ground. I waited a day too long. Damn, I waited and I knew better; I knew better than to sit around in winter letting the snow pile up in my path. I was on the trail an hour later.

Solid cloud cover blocked all light. I hiked virtually sightless. The darkness laughed at my headlamp and the twirling snowflakes reflected what little light it produced back into my eyes. I could not see the trail more than five feet ahead. Once I lifted my pack to my back, there were no discernable landmarks. Only the two big trees stood out in the storm. The snow was thick and wet, and light could only penetrate for a few feet. I looked at the two trees that marked my camp, then turned around and headed off blind in the general direction that I remembered from my approach. Before taking a step, I paused to make note of the wind on my back. Off my right hip, behind my right ear. If the wind was steady and I kept the wind there, I had a chance of staying on course to where I expected to find the crossroads. I sought closely spaced landmarks. I stopped and calibrated to the wind and hoped in vain that my night vision improved. With almost a foot of snow over the last two days, I could not feel my way along the trail with my feet. I felt little flakes of emotion strike me like snow on my face; anger for having waited, anxiety with the conditions, stress as my other senses struggled to make up for what I could not see. I moved slowly forward for what seemed a long, tense time.

Almost surprised, I saw the sign reflecting the light from my headlamp; '500 – Lolo Motorway'. It was with some relief that I found the crossroads and I took the west fork toward Indian Post Office, the next major landmark on the Lewis & Clark trail and the highest point on the path. The motorway was easier to navigate even with limited vision. The prevailing wind would be on the right side of my face; not terribly accurate until I got up toward the ridge, but a helpful tool in bad conditions. My headlamp turned snowflakes into shooting stars that flamed across my field of view and created optical chaos in the dark. I turned off the headlamp and let my eyes adjust to the night.

I moved a few steps and looked around. At times, I traveled by feel alone; I used my sticks as would a blind man following a curb. It was utterly dark that stormy morning. Even after sunrise, the thick clouds and heavy snow blotted out the sun. The light was flat. The snow accumulated rapidly. The large trees filled with inches of snow, and the small trees bent over from the weight of it to form amusing shapes and poses. I thought to stop and take pictures, but felt hurried. I tried to be mindful about taking my time because the trek was beginning to feel more serious than fun. It was a long walk to Indian Post Office and all uphill. The snow grew deeper every mile which slowed my progress significantly, and I wanted to get there before dark. I stopped only when necessary and I ate as I traveled. It started to feel like a forced march. It reminded me of some of the bigger climbs I experienced as a young man, having to stop to catch my breath every dozen yards or so. But those mountains were 14k-17k feet; Indian Post Office was half that high. I was on snow whereas the big climbs were rock.

I was about a mile away and 500' below my destination for the day. I post-holed over the middle of my calf with every step toward the Post Office. I thought about breaking out the snowshoes, but felt too close to take the time to strap them on. It was a bad decision; the trail got steeper and the snow got deeper and I was way over my calorie burn for the day. My pit zippers were open and I sweated like a boxer in a sauna. I struggled with snowdrifts up to my knees. I leaned on my poles to lift a foot out of the snow hole. I fought to maintain balance. I was elated when I finally reached the Forest Service sign identifying the Lewis & Clark landmark.

Indian Post Office

- 6966' -

But it was anticlimactic. There was a pile of rocks and a pole that poked out of the pile. There was a lot of snow. No spectators, no fans to cheer me on. No sponsors with tables of hot food and drink. Nothing but more of the same. It was, however, the objective of a difficult day and I enjoyed checking it off the list.

There was enough daylight left to set up camp. My alpine start had saved the day. I had plenty of time to dig a pit in the snow for my tent. I unstrapped the snowshoes from the pack and used them as shovels to clear out the snow. After clearing an area twice the size of my tent, I stepped into the snowshoes and stomped down the snow beneath my campsite. I unpacked my gear, placed the frozen base layer back between the pads, and fired up the stove to melt some snow for water. I hung the barometer on a branch by the tent; it was 16 degrees. Judging by the barometric pressure trend, I expected the storm to last a few days. I crawled into the tent as the sun went down. The red on the clouds was the most light I had seen that day. I knew better than to think the clouds were breaking up. There would be new snow on the ground in the morning.

I stayed the next day at Indian Post Office. It was the highest point on Lolo Trail and I wanted to wait a day for a better view. I hoped for a break in the weather. And I wanted to make time to square away my gear. I wanted to put a mile or two on my snowshoes; the snow was knee-deep and I could test drive them without my pack. Random rays of light shone through the pillowy cloud cover and created the illusion of warmth and joy. But it was numbingly cold; dangerous to the unprepared. I tread a thin line between sweating while working and freezing while sitting still. I opened the pit zippers on my jacket to make sure I did not overheat. I wore all three layers (base, mid, and outer) when exerting myself, but I did not wear my down jacket until evening when I was sitting around the campsite.

I spent the day playing around in my snowshoes and took dozens of pictures of the effects of the snow storm. Everywhere was eighteen inches of white flake piled high and sculpted into eye-popping art. Small trees transformed into small people of folklore and myth. Several tree gnomes marked my path to a field of Ents. The thick snow added shape and heft to the trees. Unfortunately, there was very little light. The sun was a pinhole in the leaden gray sky. The sky was so featureless that it blended with the ground. When I looked off the ridge, it was difficult to determine where the ground ended and the sky began. Then snow hovered in on the breeze. There was no view, no landscape to be photographed. Instead, there was the dismal wet cold encountered by Lewis & Clark.

(from the journals of Lewis & Clark - September 16, 1805 (Indian Post Office))

> "the snow in the morning 4 inches deep on the old snow, and by night we found it from 6 to 8 inches deep ... I have been wet and as cold in every part as I ever was in my life. ... men all wet cold and Hungery. Killed a Second colt which we Suped haritly on and thought it fine meat..."

There was the mental burden of gray days, lashing winds, and never-ending mountains. There was the challenge of navigating through a vast wilderness in difficult conditions. In the Selway, it took a few days for me to acclimate to living in the mountains. On that day at Indian Post Office, I acclimated to the mountains in the winter.

The next destination on my trip down Lolo Trail was the Sinque Hole. If the snow on the trail was packed down and the weather cooperative, I could cover the ten miles in daylight. Unfortunately, the snow could not possibly have been packed down and my barometer indicated no change in the weather, so it would be a long day on the trail. There were few opportunities for fresh running water this time of year, but I would pass Howard's Creek and was going to take a 1-mile roundtrip detour to fill my jug. Depending on my progress, it might be a good place to brew a cup of tea and top off my fluids.

I looked on the map and saw the obvious waypoints. Points of interest on Lolo Trail were conveniently located 8-10 miles apart. It was either Sinque Hole or the Smoking Place and I was certain the weather would be a factor. A conservative approach would be an early start toward Sinque Hole with a stop at Howard's Creek.

When I left the Indian Post Office, I knew I had a struggle ahead of me. Just like Cayuse Creek, I stayed an extra day hoping for the weather to break. In both cases, it turned out to be a bad decision; the weather got worse. And while I had already reached the highest elevation on the trail, I was not finished climbing. Hiking as a ridge-runner, I moved through the mountains by connecting peak to peak via ridges and saddles. It was never linear; I always moved up and down. Plenty of climbing remained for me. The pace slowed because of the weather, so I struck out that morning with a revised strategy of making 8 miles each day. It seemed a reasonable objective. Less than two miles down the trail, I was forced to change my plan.

Even with snowshoes on, I sank up to my calves in powder that had fallen during the night. My snowshoes were not big enough to support me and my pack. I had done the math and fudged the numbers because I wanted the 'shoes to work. But I was too big a man with too big a load for the cool little techno-shoes to carry. I worked twice as hard; I sank deeper without the snowshoes, but a boot without snowshoes extracted easier. When I sank 6-8 inches in snowshoes, I had to lift the snow-covered snowshoe out of the hole, and that wore me out. It was a big increase in cardio; it was physically taxing to balance heavy weight on my back while doing knee lifts in the snow. I wasn't in any danger; it was just going to take a lot longer to get where I was going. I hauled weight through deep powder and sank deep with every step. I ground my way up a steep section. It was not straight and I kept hoping that, at the next turn, the path leveled out or started to descend. The mental challenge was as great as or greater than the physical one. After all, the weather might turn from bad to worse. Bent over like a pack mule, I mindlessly pushed ahead. I looked up the trail to see the next turn and spotted something coming toward me down the trail. My brain short-circuited; it could not believe what I was seeing.

Like a train emerging from a gray mist in a tunnel, a snowmobile slid slowly down the slope in front of me. I stood transfixed, as some Neanderthal might ponder something impossible. Except for the lodge, I had lived more than a month without human contact. Suddenly, a human magically appeared and it was riding a motor with a light on it. He pulled up beside me, turned the motor off, and we stared at each other before speaking.

"That you post-holin' up by Post Office?" Soft-spoken but direct, the man was not unfriendly. He must have passed my camp while I was sleeping.

"Yes, sir", I puffed while I tried to catch my breath. He sounded like he could have been from Canada. Maybe Minnesota. It could have been a dream.

"You ain't the fella that's been settin' traps up by Cayuse Creek, are ya'?"

I didn't answer. I tried to act normal.

"No," he surmised, "you don't look like no trapper."

He was relaxed. Low-key... just looked at me. He was about six feet tall, medium build, dark hair. He didn't have a beard, but had not shaved lately. He wore dark green wool trousers with Stihl chain saw suspenders and a red-and-black checked wool shirt. Multiple layers were exposed at his neck and most of them looked old-school. He had big winter Pac boots and a wool hat so old – well – it must have been of sentimental value because it wouldn't warm a biscuit. It was thickly stitched of dark blue wool, and was ripped and frayed in places. His snowmobile was loaded up like an old man's RV.

There were big buckets of secret stuff on the back and a five-foot pair of Alaskan snowshoes with rawhide lacing slung off one side. It was not a junker by any means; it appeared quite practical and kitted out specifically for trapping.

"If you're not trappin', what'cha doin' up here?"

"I'm a trekker. I'm doing that Lewis & Clark thing."

"I been trappin' this state for almost 40 years and I never seen anyone trekkin' up here before. Not during trappin' season. Not in November." He took off his glove and extended his hand with a friendly grin on his face. "They call me Trapper Joe."

Trapper Joe? I recognized the name from the bar in the lodge and out in the gas station; a framed picture of him standing beside a wall of marten pelts. 300 martens harvested by one man in one season. That was a lot of work and a hell of a haul. Back in the day, a marten brought $200. A man that brought in that kind of harvest was a professional. He got up at 5 a.m. every winter's day and headed out to check his sets no matter the weather outside. In a lot of local people's minds, Trapper Joe was a living legend.

"Where ya' headed?"

"The end of the trail."

"There's lots of those…" he said.

"Lolo Trail."

"Well, I set traps all the way to Liz Butte, so I've graded it down for you that far. That's about half of what you got left."

"Thank you, sir. That's a huge help. I appreciate it."

Packing the trail down with his snow machine meant that my snowshoes would work better.

"I'm headed back to Cayuse Creek," he said and pointed back past where I had come. "Someone been runnin' a string where I been workin' since Opening Day. I'm hopin' I can talk with him, sort things out."

He wasn't angry and did not seem upset. Joe did not seem to be an angry man. But I'd wager he put value on manners and protocol, and someone was going to be schooled in free trapper protocol real soon. He fired up his snowmobile, gave me a wave, and rode slowly down the hill.

I stood stunned for a couple of minutes. If not for the evidence of the packed snow ahead of me, I would have thought the meeting a hallucination.

"Trapper Joe," I paused to consider the happenstance. "I met Trapper Joe on the Lolo Trail!" I laughed out loud at the wacky encounter and hopped on the sidewalk he paved in the snow. My pack was still heavy and the weather still bad, but I wasn't sinking as deep with every step. I stretched out my stride as best I could and headed toward Howard's Creek. I made the 1-mile detour for a drink of creek water and then resumed my labors.

A couple hours later, Joe came up the trail behind me.

"Hop on," he said. "You can come with me to camp."

"Thank you kindly, Joe, but I can't; it'd be cheating.

"Riding a snowmobile in the snow? That's cheating?" Joe looked puzzled.

"Lewis & Clark didn't have snowmobiles."

"They didn't have Gore-Tex, either!" he laughed and looked at my orange jacket. I laughed, too. It was a genuine feel-good laugh.

"Is there any water down by your camp?" I asked.

"Serpent Creek, maybe 15 yards from the tent flap. You're welcome to stay and ride out this storm. I got plenty of food and welcome good company."

"Sounds great, Joe. I'll take you up on that. Are you set up by Saddle Camp?"

I remembered Saddle Camp from my map. It was two or three miles downhill from where we stood on the route I took to the Sinque Hole.

"Yeah. Go right at the crossroads and you'll see the creek." Joe paused as he looked down at my feet buried in the snow. "And uh, you might think of tradin' those recreational snowshoes in on a pair of these." He patted the long rawhide platforms hanging underneath the seat. "You'd be floatin' up the hill with these." He stared at the dinky snowshoes under my feet, then looked up with a shake of his head. "But you're makin' it, I guess. See ya' at dinner."

Joe took off on his snowmobile and I bounced down the ridge. There wasn't much scenery because the clouds were so low, but it seemed a little less gray than before my meeting with a complete stranger. The pack weighed the same but the path was plowed and that powered me down the trail. The ridge tilted downhill and I picked up speed. I stood up into the pack (instead of leaning into the hill) and it felt good to stretch. My sticks ticked and the snowshoes slid over the track groomed by Trapper Joe.

Ninety minutes passed and I found myself at the Saddle Camp crossroads. I followed Joe's directions and turned to the right. Two hundred yards down on the left, I saw a pickup truck, a snowmobile, and a wall tent. I smiled because I knew I was about to get my first look at a right proper trapper's camp. As a mountaineer and a trekker, my camps were always minimal.

Joe had a wall tent the size of a garage and a wood-burning stove. He cooked real food. He had a cook box, a small portable cabinet, and wood stacked everywhere. Later on, he told me his Dad had started a logging company and Joe earned his share by working as a logger. And I could see the proof; when he set up his trapper camp, Joe whipped out a chain saw, felled a couple trees, and sliced them into rounds. The three-foot rounds were stacked three deep down the left side of the tent and the wall behind the stove. He had wood to last all winter.

"Wow, Joe! I can warm up while we visit in here. Can I dry out a thing or two? Where do you want me to set up?" The words bubbled out of me, one sentence led to the next. I stood up close to a warm stove and it made me feel good.

"Set up? No, you set up in here; you can throw down over in that corner. I got plenty of food and we can talk about this weather."

"That's very kind of you, Joe. But I need to complete this trek in proper style, ya' know. I got no problem sleepin' outside."

"I can respect that. Interesting project; retracing that Lewis & Clark thing."

Joe took his time when he talked. He didn't seem inclined to hurry through something as rare as conversation.

"Walkin' it on your own in November? In all my years in the backcountry, I've never seen a man doin' that. Kinda startled me, to see you head down comin' up that trail. But that's what you're doin' and you think ridin' is cheatin' the walk; I get it."

"No unnecessary assists," I confirmed.

Joe looked amused as he considered his next play.

"But what about this," he said. "Lewis & Clark are on the trail and the weather is just terrible. They are cold and wet and hungry. Not dyin' but miserable as hell. They come along a Shoshone man that knows the lay of the land, smoke curlin' up from his teepee, and food warmin' on a hot fire. You think Lewis & Clark gonna stay outside, do ya'? Or are they gonna go inside and eat?"

I had to laugh. And he laughed, too. He was so easy to be with; a welcome break in the grind. And he made sense. His argument was convincing, so I dropped my pack on the floor, pulled out my frozen long-johns, and hung them by the fire to dry. I had been granted the gift of comfort and accepted it graciously.

Trapper Joe

Joe started dinner as I unpacked my gear.

"Ya' wanna pop?"

"What?"

"A soda pop."

"Oh, a coke."

"Ain't got Coke. I got RC or a root beer."

"Root beer!? Definitely a root beer."

Joe lifted the tent flap and exposed a half dozen soda pop cans chilling in the wintry weather. The familiar dark orange and copper brown logo of a A&W Root Beer can looked beautiful with snowflakes piled on top.

"Here ya' go. Plenty more where that came from."

"Thank you, Joe. This is quite a treat."

I savored the sweet drink. My first impulse was to gulp it down, but I sipped it slowly and with great pleasure.

Joe sat by the stove. It was easy to see that he spent a lot of time alone. He did not engage in idle conversation and was thoughtful in reply. He lived within himself. There was a nice fire burning and plenty more wood for it stacked to his left within arm's reach. He sat in a folding aluminum chair, the same folding chair that he sat in all winter. He put wood in the same stove and fiddled with the same damper and relied on his work to keep his mind busy. He sat close enough to the fire that his knees were open to avoid touching the side. There was a rusty metal stovepipe venting the smoke out the side of the tent and the hot pipe was kept off the canvas with an aluminum window in the wall. Joe tended a frying pan that sat on top of the stove in which two meat patties fried. He was at home in that tent; he needed nothing more from life.

"What's that?"

"Antelope," Joe said matter-of-factly. He waited a two-count, then slowly turned to look up at me all deadpan and said, "Ever eat antelope?"

"Sure," I replied, sitting in the lawn chair reserved for guests. "I lived in Wyoming. Great herds of the silly bastards roaming around Wyoming. Can't stalk them within 400 yards, but if you lay down and wave a flag, they'll come close enough to club to death. They're too damn dumb to taste good. I've eaten antelope a couple times, but I can't say as it was very tasty."

"This is tasty," assured Joe. "Got the right spices in this and some tasty suet. We'll see if you like it. Want it on bread?"

"Lord God, you have bread?!"

Joe laughed. He turned the patties a couple of times and added wood to the fire. He fiddled with the damper, spun it to make it tighter and then to loosen it up again. A loaf of bread sat on the countertop. He put the antelope patties on paper plates and placed a big bag of

Cheetos between us on the floor. Root beer, Cheetos, and Trapper Joe's antelope burgers; life had gotten a whole lot better over the course of a single day.

We ate in silence. I chewed the food slowly, learning for the first time the real meaning of mastication. Meat juice made my mouth crazy; it took willpower to keep from wolfing down the antelope. The Cheetos were so loud, a crunchy vibration in my jaw. It wasn't cheesy, but I really liked the flavor. And the root beer; nothing beat that cold root beer. When he finished, Joe folded his plate and put it in the corner of his countertop, which was a 3' x 8' sheet of plywood laid on top of the stack of firewood. Joe split and stacked firewood along the back left side of his tent and then laid the countertop on it and the cook box at the end. Everything he needed could be reached from his seat in front of the stove. He put the frying pan back on the fire, poured some water into it, and squirted dish soap in to soak. Then he went outside.

When he came back in, he had a big mess of fur in his hands.

"Pine marten," he said as he sat down on his chair. They were adorable creatures the size of a house cat. Their fur was dark brown with a lighter streak down its back. It was called sable in other parts of the world and remained popular in the international fur market. Trapper Joe skinned those pine martens with little apparent effort. He used a small pointed knife that he honed between pelts. He was meticulous in his work, being careful to lift the eyelid off the prize and not to miss any of its lips. There was very little fat on the animal which made skinning it easier and cleaner. Joe removed the end of each of its limbs and removed the hide from the carcass in one clean pull. A small hideous meat creature with bulging eyes was tossed over by the tent flap to be added to a pile of carrion outside when the trapper finished skinning his catch. The three pelts were logged into a journal (along with location and conditions), placed into a Ziploc bag, and stored for safekeeping. Joe grabbed the ugly carcasses on his way back outside. He prepared his equipment for the next day's work; refilled his bait bucket, put fuel in the snowmobile, and covered everything with a tarp. Then he returned to the warmth of the wall tent.

Trapper Joe got out of his work clothes and hung them on a peg by the stove. The wet wool steamed and hissed when it touched the stove pipe.

"You just walkin' out of here, are ya'? Which way?" he asked. "All the way to Kooskia?"

"Yes, sir. That's the plan. I'm going to follow this motorway to Sherman's Saddle and then the old trail breaks off to the south. I plan to follow the old path down Willow Ridge, across Hungery Creek, and west out Lewis & Clark Grove. Follow logging roads from there to Kooskia and catch a ride back to Lochsa Lodge."

"Not sure there's much of a route there, Pat. A lot of those old trails are in pretty poor shape. I hear that Willow Ridge trail only goes halfway down; you might have to do some serious bushwhacking. Never been there myself. No easy day if the weather comes in. Could get kinda grim. Why don't you just follow the Lolo Motorway out to Kooskia? It's gonna snow for a couple more days yet. Could get deep out there."

"I can't, Joe. They went through Hungery Creek and west through the grove. I can't take the motorway to Kooskia."

"Yeah," he said while delivering a root beer from the under the tent flap, "takin' the easier way might be cheatin'. Wouldn't want to take the easy way." He winked in understanding but poked fun at the same time.

"There was no easy way, man. When Lewis & Clark left St. Louis in 1804, they left the world behind. There was no support; no search and rescue. They endured every kind of physical and mental hardship, one of the greatest of which was crossing these Rocky Mountains. It's spooky, knowing you've got to cross mountains for as far as the eye can see, and that far again, and again and again. Endless ass-whipping days of climbing, sweating, gasping for air and straining under loads. At least I know where it ends, man. Lewis & Clark had to think it might go on forever."

It was quiet for a minute. We sipped our soda pops and reveled in each other's company. It was a lot like any other conversation; we just paused longer before we replied.

"What about going to the moon? Don't you think that's a little bit bigger adventure than taking the Missouri to the Rockies and the Columbia to the coast? The French were already there," challenged Joe.

"I've considered that," I responded thoughtfully, setting up a volley. "But the Apollo astronauts had thousands of engineers around the world watching every detail around the clock. Lewis & Clark were on their own. Self-sufficient. Committed to success."

"Greatest adventure in our history?" Joe considered it seriously. "Maybe it was..."

"Most important adventure, for sure. They paved the way for men like you, Joe. They paved the way for trappers. And that led to lots of other business."

"I don't know; maybe that's right. They cleared the way for Americans. The Brits had Hudson Bay set up in Canada back in the 1600s. By the time Lewis & Clark came up the Missouri, trappers were already in the mountains. But not free trappers. Voyagers; company men. Those two fellas that met 'em on the way back to St. Louis, those were free trappers. Remember?"

"Hancock and Dixon," I remembered out loud. "Lewis & Clark agreed to let John Colter join them and show them the way to Three Forks. Colter left the pair after a year on the Missouri and took up with Manuel Lisa in the Bighorn Mountains in Wyoming. He was sent by Lisa to tell the Indians about the fort and invite them to bring furs and crafts to trade. That trip alone in the winter through what is now Yellowstone and Jackson Hole ranks as one of the greatest solo treks of modern times. And the fur trade grew, trappers came to the Rockies, and our country expanded West."

I tried not to get too animated, but my passion was evident as I shared my secret love with my new friend. I could hear my voice get louder and more intense.

"Didn't last long, did it… those boys trapped all the beaver out of those mountains in 25-30 years," Joe exclaimed. "A couple dozen Rendezvous and they had to move along. West, or maybe Canada."

We reflected on the heady days of free trapping in the Rockies. On 'living the life', exposed to hostiles and monstrous grizzly bears, threatened by starvation or dying of thirst, learning to live with the land and learning to read its signs. Both Joe and I were absorbed by such things and we thought the same things together.

"Didn't matter. They adapted. New games for the same old spirits. They became scouts for the Army as it opened trails for pioneers. They became lawmen in the frontier towns or prospectors when gold was found. A man's going to find adventure, Joe, if that's what's in his heart."

"And you're chasin' adventure, are ya'?" asked Joe.

"Ain't you?" I smiled.

"I don't know if I got adventure or if adventure's got me!"

We laughed and toasted, he with his RC Cola and me with my root beer. He was a real-life trapper with a camp in the Clearwater and I was going to ride the storm out in his company. It was an unexpected twist to my personal adventure and one I welcomed whole-heartedly.

We talked for a couple hours about his home in Pinehurst and the logging business built by his father. He talked about all the things he learned from his father, about logging, construction, and the great outdoors. Joe had a life outside of his life as a trapper. He trapped because he loved to; he trapped hard all winter long. He showed me pictures of him building a cabin in northern Idaho. He built it by himself. The pictures showed him lifting logs with heavy equipment (owned by his company), positioning them, setting them down, and fastening them together. Without assistance from others, Joe built a hell of a cabin.

"It's about 17 miles back and you have to carry in your groceries, so you want to get an early start."

"Sounds like a great place to spend the winter."

"It's not for everybody," Joe said, "but it's perfect for folks like us. You can use it any time you want to; just let me know before you go." Naturally shy, Joe was happy to have company for a change. There was a cot in the corner, so I figured he must get some visitors. But we were talking like two old ladies at tea.

"You want another pop?"

"No, Joe, I'm good. I'm going to brush my teeth and get ready for bed."

"Always a good idea. Nothing like sleeping with snow falling on your tent."

I walked outside to brush my teeth and looked up at the sky. There were no stars; just snowflakes as big as cotton balls falling like feathers from the sky. I paused between teeth in homage to the beauty of winter in the mountains. The north wind kept the arctic chill on, but the clouds helped hold in the heat. I spat the mint foam out on the ground. I rinsed my mouth out and spat again. I had a bedtime pee and went inside.

"You got that corner in the front. Yeah, that one. That's Cole's cot; you can use it if you want."

It didn't look like a cot. It looked like it might have been a cot at one time. Now it was more like a pile of cot bones scattered in the corner. I opted for my standard twin pad set-up; the closed-cell egg carton-looking one on the bottom and the open-cell self-inflating air mattress on top. I topped it with my high loft sleeping bag and looked around at Joe as I posed by my high-tech cocoon. Joe stood at the back of the tent on the side opposite the stove. There was a large bedroll at his feet and it was a lot bigger than mine. It was held in place by two straps with quick lock snaps. When he unbuckled the straps, a huge sandwich of bed linens rolled out across the floor. There was an 8" foam rubber mattress on the bottom which was covered by sheets and a blanket. Then there was a wool blanket, of course, and a comforter. Two pillows sprung free from the roll to complete the full-size-bed-in-the-woods effect. I was blown away. My bedding, though high-tech, suddenly seemed woefully insufficient. Lewis & Clark had wall tents and bedrolls, but they had horses to carry the loads. Joe had his pickup to carry a truck full of comfort and food. I had ultralight gear and snowshoes that sank in the snow. I dragged the lawn chair to my bedside and humbly began to remove my boots. Minutes later, the lights were doused and two old youngsters went to sleep.

It snowed hardest that next day. Joe's alarm went off at 5 o'clock in the morning. He threw the dirty paper plates from the day before into the stove along with some kindling and diesel fuel. He lit it and we had fire. The tent warmed up quickly. He boiled up some coffee and cooked sausage and hash browns for breakfast. It was glorious.

Joe made a short run to check his sets and trapped three more marten that morning. We spent most of that stormy day getting to know each other. He was pleasantly surprised to learn that I spent the prior month roaming the Selway. He spent a lot of time there and asked about the conditions of several areas, especially Big Sand Lake. It was a favorite to both of us. He made recommendations for future excursions and shared his experiences in that remote wilderness. His knowledge was vast and he was generous with it.

In the afternoon, I picked his brain about trapping. How does one set a trap? What do you use as bait? Is bait the same as lure? How do you know where to set them? He opened up as our relationship developed, but one of the best trappers in all of Idaho was slow to give up his secrets. And one of them would not be shared. Still, I learned a lot on that day in the tent with Trapper Joe. It was more than coincidence. It was a meaningful encounter.

Later in the day, we broke out the topographic maps and explored every detail of my route. He pointed out areas of potential trouble; areas that could be dangerous if the snow came in to stay. He provided detail that could not be gleaned from maps and suggestions that only a few knew enough to make. He felt that I should stay on the motorway to the end of the trail in Kooskia. He felt the historic route was in disrepair and sections did not exist.

"The fat historians that wrote those books you read didn't go roamin' too far off the trail, my friend. And this ain't no time of year to be bushwhackin', either. You look like you're in good shape, but bein' fit ain't always enough to get you to the other side."

The guidebook for the Lolo Trail offered a similar opinion; the author said no government funding was earmarked for trail maintenance. But no one maintained the trail taken by the Corps of Discovery, either, and I was alright with finding my way.

Joe got up and looked out the flap at the relentless storm.

"I got to move my truck down if it don't get better soon," he casually remarked while staring blankly at the white.

"What?" I was incredulous. He had a huge 4-wheel drive truck literally customized for the high country.

"All it takes is a 2'-3' drift and that truck could be stuck here 'til the spring. If it gets deep, I move the truck down and use the snow machine to move camp. I only have to go as far down as it takes to turn to rain."

After dinner, I fiddled with my gear and Joe shared from his experiences. He sat by the fire and spun the damper in and out, telling me about growing up in Idaho. He slipped a stick or two of firewood in the stove as soon as there was room for it. He wasn't a self-centered person; he shared and made every effort to be hospitable. He told me that he set his first trap at ten, got serious at 16, and had been trapping ever since. Mostly he just trapped pine martens because they always brought a good price. He had trapped most everything at one time or another, but he had focused on pine marten the last few years. He also told me that there was a fair amount of gold in Idaho and he'd done a bit of prospecting. He'd gone up north to the mouth of the St. Joe and done some sluice work there.

One thing that stuck with me was a story about his dad. Joe was getting ready for the trapping season and his father advised him to wait a few weeks 'til December to 'cabin trap' (where a trapper circulates between three cabins to check sets every three days). He said that the deep snows of December would cover all the scrub brush and small trees, and only the tallest trees would stand out against the snow-covered landscape.

"You want to see something special? Put on your long snowshoes and go walk through those treetops when the moon is bright. It's like walking on another world." It was a great visual to take to bed that night. We crashed early for an early start.

Bacon and flapjacks! It was the first thing I smelled when I woke up. My first conscious thought was 'that beats the hell out of a half-cup of oats'. I got out of my bag, stuffed it in the stuff sack, and stuffed it in my pack.

"So you leavin', are ya'?" Joe asked as he poured coffee.

"Gotta go, Joe. I appreciate your generosity and I'm happy for the company, but I need to finish this trek before the snow comes in for good." I looked out at the cold mist falling from the dense cloud cover. It hadn't warmed up much but the barometer rose; I figured 12-16 hours before the high pressure actually moved in.

"Let me ask you one question," then he paused. "You gotta be somewhere, do ya'? Got an appointment in town or some such?"

He looked at me over his coffee cup which he had lifted to his lips to cool.

"Well, no, Joe. Not exactly." I smiled at his way of making a point.

"The Indians call it 'three sleeps', but it's two full days, really. That's the tradition. You've only been here for two sleeps and this is the start of the second full day, which is a small percentage of the time you'll spend on this trail. The storm has passed and the weather is getting better, but it won't be nice 'til tomorrow. If you want to stay until this storm moves out, you are welcome. I left two root beers by the flap and you can help yourself to the food. I'll be back in a few hours. And if you decide to leave, take the root beers and my contact info. I left it on the cook box. It's been a great couple days, either way. Gotta go." He straddled his machine, waved goodbye, and rode off to do a trapper's work.

He was right, of course. One more day would not matter. I looked at my barometer and saw three bars had risen. The way I figured, it should clear off at night and tomorrow would be a great day for hiking. I shook my head and smiled at the serendipity of it all; that I would meet a trapper while reliving the trip that opened to door to free trapping in the West.

I split wood for a couple hours to replenish the supply under the countertop. There were two sizes of wood; 1" lathes used as kindling and 2"-3" pieces to burn for fuel. I filled the space under the plywood and then toted water from Serpent Creek to fill the big Igloo cooler in the tent. Then I sat down, started a fire, and took a root beer from the tent flap. I broke out my journal and caught up with the last few days. I looked over the maps again and reconsidered my options at Sherman Saddle. It looked to be a critical decision and my good sense told me something different than my heart was saying. My heart said to follow the Corps, but common sense said to stay on the motorway.

Joe came in late in the day. He looked the way that he always looked; happy to be trapping and having a good day.

"So guess what I caught in my traps today?" he beamed when I met him as he pulled up outside.

"Hunting dogs?"

"No."

"Pine martens?"

"Yes. And how many pine martens did I trap today?" he asked, bursting with understated pride.

"Well, Joe, I believe you're going to get 100 martens out of here this month. That means you've got to average more than three martens a day."

"Guess I got two-and-a-half days' worth!" he exclaimed. He used both hands to hold up his catch for the day. Seven martens and one ermine.

"Damn, man! That's incredible. What's that white one?"

"That's an ermine. It's a weasel in the winter. They don't bring much, especially if they're small. That's a whole mess a' marten, though. Real good day out there today."

He was genuinely pleased at his success. It wasn't the money, although it added up to a nice chunk of change. It was the primal sport of it. Trapping was a game where man tried to outsmart animal. Joe outsmarted the martens regularly and there was an instinctive satisfaction in that. My new friend was the real thing; a free trapper in the wilds of Idaho. There can be no substitute for that experience, for the time I spent with Joe. He bridged the gap between my ideas of the trappers of the 1830s and the 21st century mountain man. He sparked my fertile imagination and I appreciated that.

He skinned marten for the next two hours and tended to the business of trapping. There were sandwiches for dinner and a couple hours' conversation to fill the rest of the evening. Joe was pleased with his catch that day. We ate sugar cookies, Flaming Cheetos, and drank pop, and he fiddled with the damper on the fire. I felt free to be myself around Joe and he felt the same about me. Not bad for a chance meeting in the literal middle of nowhere.

I woke up a little after 4 a.m. to take a leak and the thermometer read 17 degrees. I looked at the sky and saw stars for the first time in a week. I went back inside the tent and started to gear up. Joe made coffee, bratwursts, and hash browns. We ate, exchanged numbers, and went outside to take a couple of pictures together. I put on my snowshoes when Joe came up to me and said,

"Hey, trekker. You figured out we got no grizzlies in this country? Nothing here gonna do you any harm. Maybe you oughta leave that heavy pistol here. I'll wrap it up good and leave it with Mike down at the lodge. You can pick it up when you pack back out. Save you 6 pounds. Damn near 10% of your pack weight, right?"

"Damn, Joe, you're thinking like a trekker, man. I like it," I said and pulled the holster off my chest. "That's a great idea."

"I'll leave it with Mike down at the store at the lodge. It will be there when you get back."

"Thanks, Joe. Thanks for everything. I'll catch up with you later."

"Hey, one more thing; somewhere down the south end of Willow Ridge is supposed to be an old cabin. They call it Obia's Cabin; somewhere east of Obia's Point. Don't know where it is exactly and no one that I know does. Since you seem hell-bent on goin' down around that way, I thought I'd bring it up. Doubt you'll run across ol' Obia's Cabin, but I'd be interested to know what kind of shape it's in. If you find it, that is."

"Obia's Cabin. Will it have a sign on it?"

"Hell, I don't even know if it is still standing. Never seen it; it's just a rumor. But you're headin' that way and most folks don't. Just keep an eye out, that's all."

I waved and he waved, and I struck out on the trail again.

After the Storm

After three sleeps and two full days at Joe's camp, I finally stepped back onto the Lolo Trail. There were clouds in the sky, but they were scattered and blue skies opened up the vistas once again. I could see for miles and miles. Everywhere the mountains were covered with snow. Even the tall trees had as much snow as they could hold on their branches. It gave them a heaviness that would last the season.

Joe ran three trap lines out of Saddle Camp; one back up Cayuse Creek, one up the road past Howard's Creek, and a long one west of the camp at Liz Butte. The snowmobile track to Liz Butte followed Lolo Motorway and made my travel easier, but it had filled in during the storm. I knew Joe would check that set tomorrow and his snowmobile would pack a sidewalk all the way to Sherman's Saddle (where the road peeled off toward Liz Butte). In the meantime, I slid through the snowy track for miles and was most grateful for it. The sunshine lifted my spirits and I had a lot to be thankful for; my chance meeting with Trapper Joe felt more like a cosmic acquaintance. It gave me a lot to think about as I stretched my legs out on Lolo Trail.

From Saddle Camp, I headed due west for a couple miles until I reached the Sinque Hole. The trail turned into a long confused spiral staircase and wound its way up and around until I circled the landmark and headed south. The trail turned to the right down a long ridge that pointed southwest. Less than two miles later, I stood in the sunlight and looked up at the pile of stones called The Smoking Place. It was a most interesting place and signified more than just a stop on the road.

Legend had it that, after completing their trip west, Lewis & Clark solicited help from the Nez Perce Indians for the return trip through the mountains; they weren't particularly happy with the old Shoshone guide that led them west the year before. The Nez Perce agreed to help and led the party from the Wieppe Prairie to Lolo Mountain in Montana. Apparently, they were impressive guides.

(from the journals of Lewis & Clark – June 27, 1806 (The Smoking Place))

"short of the encampment we halted by the request of the Guides, a few minutes on an elevated point and Smoked a pipe. on this eminence the nativs a conic mound of Stons of 6 or 8 feet high and erected a pine pole of 15 feet long... from this place we had an extensive view of Stupendous Mountains principally Covered with Snow; we were entirely surrounded by those mountains from which to one acquainted with them it would have Seemed impossible ever to escape. In short, without the assistance of our guides I doubt much that we who had once passed could find our way to Traveler's Rest.

those indians are most admirable pilots; we find the road wherever the snow has disappeared though it be only for a few paces. after having Smoked the pipe and Contemplating this Scene Sufficient as any except Such hardy travelers as we have become, we continued our march."

It was almost a holy place. I carefully climbed up the pile of rocks to take in the majestic view. There was very little wind and the clear air made the mountains stand out in the distance. The view to the southeast was grand; the Nez Perce navigators must have had the wind at their backs as they shared the pipe and the view with Lewis & Clark. I climbed down to the trail but tried not to be in a hurry. After all, I had been moving for a few hours. I decided The Smoking Place would be a fine place for a break, so I dropped my pack on the ground. I opened the top to get out some jerky. Lo and behold! An original A&W Root Beer magically appeared under the flap of my pack.

"Trapper Joe, you ol' scamp!" I shouted to the mountains. "Who in the hell does that?"

I stood up with a hop of surprise and unbridled happiness.

"You crazy old coot," I said, shaking my head. "You put a root beer in my backpack!"

I danced a jig as my grin cracked the ice off my whiskers. I held the can up to look at it. It was cold to the touch. I sat down at the base of The Smoking Place and popped the top on my root beer, barely able to contain myself.

"Here's to ya', Joe. You just made this man's day!"

I did not sip the soda slowly at The Smoking Place that day. I chugged it down like beer on a hot summer afternoon. I drank it so hard and fast that it frothed in my neck. The froth expanded upward past the root beer flowing down and my nose hole filled with foam. I did not choke, however, as I stayed focused on gulping it down, increasing the expansion of the carbonated gases and the injection of sugar into my system. I sucked the bottom out of the root beer can as foam and cola spilled out of my pie hole and became sticky ice in my beard. It was easily the best root beer I ever had and I was o! so glad for Trapper Joe.

I released a great belch. I stomped the words 'Thx Joe!' in the snow bank for him to see when he rode by. I was lifted by his gesture. That little treat would last me all day; it added to the quickness in my step and the lightness in my heart. I cinched up my pack and headed out down the ridge with a smile. The sugar buzz would last for hours.

Maybe it was my amplified attitude, but the weather was as beautiful as it had been since I started my trip on the Lolo Trail. Wisps of thin stratus clouds lazed about, but the sky was mostly blue. I saw other mountains. The vantage point along the ridge provided me a view of many lesser mountains and ridgelines all covered with trees and snow. The storm had covered everything with a beauty mask for sleep. There were round red berries that grew in clusters, several clusters caused a thin gray branch to bend. A small grove of the red berry trees leaned in the same direction and seemed to point the way ahead. Behind them a line of evergreens stood erect and many times taller than the tiny berry trees. The evergreens stood against a background that appeared to be a sea of trees, rolling waves of frosted green. Clouds malingered in the lower elevations and could be looked down upon from positions on the ridge. The bright red berries in the snow against a backdrop of green and breath-taking grandeur made me stop and set up some pictures. I was fully immersed in the landscape.

The rest of the trip towards Sherman Saddle was full of well-known Lewis & Clark landmarks; Castle Butte, Dry Camp, No-See-Ums Meadows, and Sherman Saddle. Some of the sites mark the Corps of Discovery's trail west and others mark their trip home with the Nez Perce. They were all cool to me; I could see what they had seen. The mountains had not changed much in the past 200 years.

At 3 o'clock, I stopped at the turn-off to Castle Butte Lookout. The turn-off provided a large flat area for setting up camp and I stomped down a big square. I got a little carried away and stomped down a campsite the size of half a tennis court. I even stomped out a little trail to a stand of trees for a latrine. The snow all around the site was pristine; no sign of any kind. It was almost a great winter campsite. All it lacked was water.

When there was no running water, I had to make water from snow and that required a lot of heat. Fuel was an important consideration on long trips. Normally, I used very little fuel in my stove. I boiled water every morning for oatmeal and tea. It took about three minutes to boil a liter of water for my morning meal and that was all the fuel I used for the day. At that usage rate, the fuel canister would last three weeks. I didn't cook a lot of food, but I used a lot of water. If I couldn't find running water, I melted snow and made water. It took three or four times as long to melt snow as it did to cook breakfast. I loathed wasting fuel and held out in hopes of finding a creek or stream. Unfortunately, there were not many creeks or streams on the ridgelines, so I melted snow at Castle Butte. My stove was the size of a small coffee can and I scooped up snow in it, packed it down, and kept scooping until it was full. A fully packed pot melted down to less than a third of its volume. I added more and more snow until I had a quart of drinking water. I let it cool and, since I did not let it boil, I pumped it through the filter for safety's sake. Once I filled my bottle, I boiled some water for tea.

The wind had settled. The night was clear and I sat out to watch the stars. I had enjoyed Joe's company, but I loved being alone. The moonlight reflected brightly off the snow-covered landscape and the night was like daytime to me. The sugar buzz from the root beer had long since faded, but I was energized by a great day on the trail. And the sky seemed so dark compared to the sky around a city. The stars stood out like drawings in a book on astronomy. I could see the Milky Way. I lost track of time; I might have stayed up all night, but figured I needed sleep for the rough trail ahead. I finally went to bed and fell asleep immediately.

I packed quickly in the morning and headed out for Bald Mountain. The high pressure cell hovered over me like a protective mother. The sun was out and the light splashed off the white crust on the trees. In a couple of miles, I saw it glaring off the dome of Bald Mountain. They called it Bald Mountain because, unlike other mountains in the area, there were no trees on top. I figured it would be deep in new snow and that it would take a lot of time to get past. I planned to take my time and make No-See-Ums Meadows by the end of the day. It wasn't overly ambitious, but the week before left a lot of snow on the ground and I thought travel would be slow. As I covered the two miles from Castle Butte cut-off to Bald Mountain, I found the snow had settled. Not packed, but settled enough to allow my snowshoes to float. And the view, unobstructed by trees, was spectacular. Clouds hid in the pockets between ridges and looked like fog-covered lakes from above. They were everywhere. They filled in open areas below 4000'. The world was turned upside down and the clouds were now below me.

Up ahead, I heard the sound of a snowmobile. Joe was coming back from his run to Liz Butte. Like the day I met him, he must have passed early before I got up to break camp. He slowed down as he approached, for being cautious was his nature.

"Hello there," he said as he slowed to a stop. He pulled the tips of the fingers of his gloves to get them off his hands. He rolled the tattered blue cap off his head and looked out over the snowy ridges.

"Beautiful day for a walk."

"Better day for a ride," he countered.

"I appreciate the trailblazing, Trapper Joe. That will make things a little easier."

"I took it out to Liz Butte," he explained. "Right about the time you come up on Sherman's Saddle, you'll hit this big S turn in the road.

Goes left for a hundred yards or more and then goes right. To Kooskia," he winked. "I got you right up to that first turn. You'll see where I went around in circles and make sure you look out for a low-hanging branch right there. You go down to that right turn and you'll see Burn Creek. Good fresh running water there. I know you like your creek water, so that's a good place to be. Maybe a good place to camp. It's right on the road but shouldn't be anyone coming up."

"I'll do that, Joe. I reckon I'll make good time today. You see my message up by the Smoking Place?"

"Where you found the root beer?" he chuckled. "Yeah, I saw that."

He put the hat back on his head. He was low-key and not prone to showing a lot of emotion.

"You take care now, Pat Taylor. I'll see you around. Maybe at the lodge when you're finished. I'll meet you there for breakfast."

"See you later, Joe." With that, we set off on separate adventures. I didn't know if I would ever see him again, but I knew for sure that I would never forget him.

The snow was packed; the sunlight had helped it to settle and my snowshoes traveled well on the track. I moved through the miles at an encouraging clip. I reached No-See-Ums Meadow shortly before lunchtime. I decided to carry on toward Sherman's Saddle but took some time for lunch at the well-known landmark. Of course, none of the landmarks appeared as they did in the guidebooks. The guidebooks were not written for winter trekking. I had a sip or two of water, some jerky, and a handful of trail mix before I pounded down the trail to Sherman's Saddle. I felt strong, buoyant, and enduring. I began to seriously consider the options that awaited me ahead.

Somewhere near Sherman's Saddle, the original Lewis & Clark trail departed from the Lolo Motorway. The motorway continued in a southwesterly direction until it reached the village of Kooskia on the western edge of the Rockies. The route reportedly followed by Lewis & Clark – the Lolo Trail – went south down the next ridge west of Sherman Saddle. It traveled down Willow Ridge until it connected with Hungery Creek (original spelling in the Lewis & Clark journals), which would be forded before taking the trail to the right (to the west) to Hungery Creek Camp. The Lolo Motorway would be easier and safer in the event of another storm, but I came to Idaho to follow Lewis & Clark through the Rockies and that required me to follow their route. I had the night to think about it. I clipped along at a good pace on my way to Sherman's Saddle. Joe said to go to the 'S' turn for a good campsite and water, so that's what I would do.

The slope was all downhill when I came off of Bald Mountain. I zoomed down Joe's fresh track on a straight run. The slope was markedly steeper and I felt the pounding in my quadriceps and knees. They pumped with blood to meet the challenge and propelled me down the ridge. Even after passing Sherman's Peak on the left, the track twisted and turned but never lost slope. It felt as though I was skiing on snowshoes during one section of the trail. Joe's snow machine left a 20" wide walkway pressed down in a couple of feet of snow. I stayed in the track on turns to avoid the risk of falling. It was great fun, almost running down a ridge line not far from the back of beyond. I moved downhill so I was not pressed for breath. The pack was not a conscious burden. I had miles of ground to cover and sat back to enjoy the ride. I stepped outside the physical to enjoy a higher perspective.

The motorway moved from the southerly side of the ridge through a saddle to the northerly side of the ridge. It was darker there and less sunlight meant more snow and ice. The last mile wove in and out of the shadows on the north side of the ridge line until I came upon the turn. I stopped before I reached it. I saw the road turn sharply left and soon disappeared behind a rock outcropping. However, I saw it re-emerge a couple hundred yards ahead after a hidden right turn following the left.

It was Joe's 'S' turn and I stopped to have a look around. Things would change a bit after this point. The 'S' turn was the end of the trail for Joe, so I would have to work harder to get through the unpacked snow. I kept a good pace although the storm cost me a few days, but there was a long way to go to the end of the trail. I walked up slowly to see around the turn, more curious than tentative. And I looked for the low-hanging limb. As I got closer to the turn, I saw something but it didn't look like a limb. It looked like a grotesquely burnt branch pointing out my path. Something unidentifiable, at least until I walked up within arm's reach.

Joe had tied a black garbage bag to a tree limb on the edge of the motorway. He tied it head high with #9 wire and he wrapped the wire around the branch many, many times. It took forever to get the bag out of the tree and I could imagine him laughing at all the work it took to open the surprise. When I finally removed the wire and plastic wrapping, I grinned with anticipation. I stood in the undisturbed center of Joe's snowmobile spinning frenzy. Apparently, he cut donuts with his snowmobile and marked the end of his trail by slinging snow around in a great big circle. The road was just a mess of snow pushed off to the side in a circle, but the commotion stopped at the corner. Down by the next turn, a creek came down that was crisp and clean and tucked into the corner. The road zig-zagged and, in the corner, Burn Creek bubbled down from above. Then it disappeared under the road.

It was mid-afternoon when I stepped off Joe's snowmobile tracks and onto the featureless track that led to the next big decision. I stopped with the sack in my hand and stood in the turn with clean water falling, and looked down the track towards Sherman's Saddle. I felt it was safe to camp there on the motorway where it was flat and had good water nearby. I knew visitors were highly unlikely, but I felt compelled to build my camp as close to the water and as removed from the motorway as possible. I placed my snowshoes as boundary markers and supplemented them with my trekking poles. Inexplicably, my instincts were on alert and I wanted to make sure that I slept safe in my tent. I unpacked only the basics; my bedding, stove, and food sack. And my maps. I looked over the area outside my tent, tossed the black gift bag inside, and turned in before it got dark.

Finally, I opened the black sack that Joe left on the trail for me. Gazing into the bag, I smiled as I beheld a cornucopia of carbs. It was manna from Heaven. I found cookies, a bagel, and flaming Cheetos. There were two root beers, a half bag of sugar wafers, a mangled chunk of banana bread, and Granny's energy cookies. I sat on the floor and munched on the bagel. I couldn't believe my good fortune. I couldn't believe ol' Joe! I had scarcely swallowed the last bite of bagel when I immediately started eating the sugar wafers two-at-a-time. They were pink and crisp and chock full of sugar, and I felt energy spikes with every crunchy mouthful. While a guest in someone's house, a certain amount of restraint must be exercised. Alone in my tent with the goody bag, I was free to eat with abandon. I drank water to try to flush out the sugars and went outside for a refill.

That's when I heard the plane crashing.

The engine was clear, easy to hear, which meant it must have been close to the ground. It kept revving up, as if it tried to gain speed, tried to climb, but then the throttle fell off unexpectedly. It seemed to sputter and struggle to fly, but the intermittent bursts of speed would not sustain its flight. It sounded like a motorcycle falling from the sky. It sounded bad and it sounded close.

"A motorcycle?" I thought. "Nah, not out here. That's ridiculous."

I listened more. I scanned the sky. It was a little too close for comfort and sounded like it was getting closer. It actually gave me the creeps. It vroom-vroom'd like a motorcycle, like someone playing with the throttle. And that's when it hit me; at the exact moment the answer came to my mind, I saw a man standing up on a snowmobile and he was coming up Lolo Motorway.

The encounter at Sherman Saddle had a completely different vibe to it than the one I had with Joe. Not a bad vibe, but I wasn't overly talkative when the man stopped his machine. He was from Kooskia; that much was obvious. He wore wind pants over jeans and a couple of sweaters, so he planned on being home that night. He stood on a brand new snow machine and he drove differently than Joe, more like a kid on a JetSki. I guessed the sounds I heard were this citizen hot-dogging his new machine out on the Forest Service trail. I realized it was Clearwater National Forest now and he had every right to ride a snowmobile, but I was almost annoyed at the disturbance.

"Wow. I didn't expect to see anyone. What are you doing out here?" he asked. He didn't ask for my name and I didn't ask for his, either.

"I'm camping," I replied as I wiped sugar cookie dust from my beard. "Hope you can get by. I had a feeling you were coming, so I tried to leave room for you to pass."

"Yeah, sure, no problem. I'm just breaking in this new machine. Got a cabin up by Liz Butte and my buddies are coming out for the weekend. I got to make sure it's in good shape."

He stood on top of his snow machine and I stood outside my tent. I must have been a sight; no bath in a couple weeks and pink sugar cookie crumbs on my face. Not to mention the crazy sugar-dilated what-the-hell-are-you-doing-here eyes.

"Where'd you come from?" I asked.

"Kooskia," he replied.

Kooskia. Whoa. The man had ridden here from Kooskia? Meaning he paved the trail all the way to Kooskia? Right up to within 200 yards of where Joe's trail ended? So by some magical passing of Fate's wand, the rest of the motorway was packed all the way to the end.

The mystery of the event dawned on me slowly and I looked at the rider with some wonder. He was middle-aged and fit. Medium-length hair and a thick mustache. He wasn't dressed like a mountain man and there weren't a lot of middle class people in the tiny village of Kooskia. He looked like one of the few.

"Well, I better be going. I'll be back this way in a couple hours."

"I'll probably be asleep. Don't run over me."

"No problem," he said. And off he went to Liz Butte.

How was I to interpret that sign? Was the unexpected rider a gift? Was he sent to pack a trail to safety? It could be no coincidence that he rode up to the very spot where Joe's track reached its end. Perhaps it was a sign to stay on the Lolo Motorway and take the easy way back to the road. And the safe way, if another storm came in.

Or was it just Chance? It was the only motorway open to traffic in that winter; anyone out on a snowmobile was going to be on that road. The rider was bringing a group on the weekend. It wasn't a sign at all, only an interesting coincidence that could be worked to my advantage. I looked up the trail where the man had ridden and where his trail overlapped Joe's. I turned to my left to look at the packed trail back to Kooskia. It was eerie, really. I laughed nervously to myself.

"I don't give a good goddam what signs might appear in these mountains," I asserted. "I came here to walk in the footsteps of Lewis & Clark and that is what I intend to do."

With resolve and no small amount of indignation, I went inside to gorge myself on what remained of the goody bag. Twice I went outside to guzzle root beer so I wouldn't mess my tent with sugar foam, but inside was a cloud of Cheeto flame powder, sugar wafer dust, and other things I ate without really looking. For a few minutes, all my self-discipline vanished. The strict diet, the Spartan approach to trail life in general – gone. I had metaphorically soiled myself in a processed food frenzy and lay nearly comatose for hours.

When I woke in the early light before the day, I used some time for planning. Emotionally, I had committed to the Lewis & Clark trail, but prudence demanded I fully consider the alternative. It was late in the year; too late for mistakes. After brewing a cup of tea, I reviewed my options on my topo maps and my GPS device.

The Corps of Discovery reportedly went south around Sherman's Saddle following Willow Ridge to get to Hungery Creek. They crossed the creek and proceeded west to Hungery Camp.

(from the journals of Lewis & Clark - September 18, 1805 (Hungery Camp)

> "The want of provisions together with the dificuely of passing those emence mountains dampened the spirits of the party which induced us to resort to Some plan of reviving ther Sperits. I deturmined to take a party of the hunters and proceed on in advance to Some leavel Country, where there was game, kill some meat & Send it back, &c"

They made their way from Hungery Creek to Portable Soup Camp, to Full Stomach Camp, and on to Lewis & Clark Grove. From there, it was only a few miles to the Weippe Prairie where the great mountains emptied out to the west. It did not sound easy. But the problems didn't sound like navigation problems; it seemed more like conditions, the time of year. And the journal made it clear that they went by way of Hungery Creek.

If all went well, I could be out of the Rockies in less than a week. I planned to follow the path and finish out on the logging roads that would take me to Kooskia when I got past the Grove. The Lolo Motorway followed the same general direction but bypassed many of the landmarks along the Lewis & Clark trail. That made the Lolo Trail all the more desirable.

Unfortunately, there were several problems with the Lolo Trail and they could prove quite serious. The leading authority on the subject, former United States Forest Service Supervisor of the Clearwater National Forest Ralph Space, wrote a book on the Lolo Trail. He stated clearly that sections of the trail were unmaintained and there was no budget in the foreseeable future. And that book was published several years ago. In laymen's terms, Mr. Space meant the going could be tough; mostly in the form of obstacles like rock slides and tree fall. Obstacles that slow one down in a place where storms could prove disastrous. As I considered my options, one thing became dangerously clear; I wasn't in the Selway anymore.

Sherman's Saddle

Things felt different when I geared up that morning. Certainly, the sugar buzz had a lingering effect. I felt more focused; more intense. I felt ready to crank it up a notch. I knew a few people who might go camping in the winter and maybe a couple who might go out for a week. But I only knew one who would go where I was going that day and I was thrilled with the prospect of my solo adventure. After spending more than a week on the Lolo Motorway, I was excited to veer off in search of the original Lewi & Clark route. I watered up at Burn Creek, took a leak, and hit the trail like a Marine on a mission.

I followed the snowmobile trail for almost half a mile. Then, off to the left of the motorway, I spotted a half-hidden trail breaking off to the side. I paused to look down at the snowmobile path to Kooskia, then turned to focus on finding a way up to Willow Ridge. I turned left up through an opening into the hillside. I found a Forest Service trail marker a few yards up the path and knew I turned at the correct place. Unlike Wendover Ridge, Willow Ridge required a more circular approach. On Wendover Ridge, I started at the bottom and climbed diagonally up the side to its top. I zig-zagged on switchbacks a few times, but it was basically just up the side.

On Willow Ridge, however, I had to circle around the north end to attack it from the west. Once on the west side, I cut back up to the ridgeline and turned right to go south along the top for several miles until it dropped off into Hungery Creek. The ridge itself ran north-to-south and I wanted to travel it to the Hungery Creek crossing. That was the provisional plan. I considered it provisional because the map showed the trail disappearing a little less than halfway down the ridge. Closer inspection of the GPS device confirmed the anomaly which sparked a noticeable measure of anxiety. And, of course, the map and GPS data corresponded with what Ralph Space had to say about the route. It could be that I was about to embark on a most frustrating and futile search. Or it could be the great adventure waiting to be lived. It could be Lewis & Clark used a different ridge which should be easy to see from the top. They were master navigators; all I had to do was get high enough to see what they would have seen. I could guess where they might have gone from there.

As I started up the hill, I looked at the snow for some clues. Initially, the trail wasn't too hard to find. A gentle indentation, a bobsled run for bunnies, a scooped-out place to step. Over the previous weeks, I had developed an eye for finding trails where they had all but disappeared. I felt strong and confident, and enjoyed the challenge of trail-finding. The path changed as it wove in and out of sunlight and shade and tight wooded areas where the trail grew constricted, and the open snow meadow where it was just the high side of a drift. Fresh game sign on the ground reminded me that not everything was asleep in winter. After a couple miles, I circled the knob and climbed to the north end of the ridge.

At the high point, I stood at about 6400'; the creek I intended to cross was four miles south and about 3200' down, and most of that drop-off was at the end. As a matter of fact, the topographical map indicated that the south end was a very steep drop; too steep to negotiate on foot and certainly too steep for stock. The ridge ran to the south; the views to the east and west were open from the ridgeline. And the view was a fine reward for a long morning's work. I was pleased as I snowshoed south along the west side of the ridge in hopes of finding a way to Hungery Creek. I looked around in observation. I studied the mountains and ridgelines around me. I looked for higher planes, connections to places easier to travel, ridges linked together by Lewis & Clark.

I looked down the narrow back of Willow Ridge and struggled with the notion of descending to the creek. I became more concerned about the exit from the ridge because I did not see a pathway west. As the trail neared the crest of the ridge, the snow deepened with a crusty layer on top. I placed a snowshoe on it and it seemed to take my weight, and then I broke through up to my knees in stiff powder. That started happening about the time the trail disappeared.

Bushwhacking through deep crusty snow slowed my progress tremendously. While I struggled with the simple act of putting one foot in front of the other, I had to pass back-and-forth in search of the disappearing trail. Forward progress came to an abrupt end as I looked for the trail that apparently vanished into the thin air. It was not unexpected; the guide book and maps matched what was happening. I went back up the trail and looked to the sides. I zig-zagged hoping to intersect something I could follow. Finally, I came across a Forest Service marker pole located approximately where my GPS showed the end of the trail. I let that soak in for a minute. It was not as comforting as it should have been. I was uncertain and more than a little uncomfortable. The confidence I left camp with that morning had disappeared somewhere behind me on the trail.

I looked back on my tracks; it would be easy to follow them downhill back to the Lolo Motorway. It was more than a little tempting. I had every good reason to do it and plenty of good reasons not to proceed. But it was getting late, so I stopped where I was and looked for a place to camp. I was physically and mentally tired, and it made sense to make camp. I found a critter bed at the base of a tree on the western side of the ridge. Sleeping critters (like moose or elk) melted the snow and ice around the base of a tree when they slept and left a warm bed of pine needles on the ground. Though they were not always flat. I wrapped my tent around the big tree and slept on a slanted critter bed that night. I tried to lay flat in my bag but kept sliding down into a tight corner of the tent. I felt like water being poured into the corner of a baggie. I slept poorly and started the morning a little bit worse for wear. Actually, a lot worse.

Stubborn, sore, and almost mad, I broke camp and kept the ridge on my left, to the east. For all I knew, there was no trail to Hungery Creek or to Hungery Camp. They might just be lines on a map placed by some fat academic who thought they should be there. Someone with theories but no practical experience. I could almost see Joe shaking his head.

But I had committed to the adventure and would do better to concentrate on solving the problem at hand. Trail or no trail, I wanted to exit Willow Ridge as close to Hungery Creek as possible. I knew I wanted to stay up on the ridge for the first mile or two and then start moving downhill to my right to steer toward Hungery Creek, which I imagined was maybe three miles away. But I needed to be down by the creek before I reached the end of the ridge; there was no safe way off of it. Theoretically, I needed to descend with the contours of the slope except that the contours looked perilously steep around the entire face of the ridge. And the ground was covered with more than a foot of snow hiding the rocks and low-lying brush that covered the hillside.

My snowshoes had performed well the day before, but the metal cleats were useless on the alder and willow branches under the snow. They did not grip but slid along the slick bark every time I stepped on them. To make matters worse, the west side of the ridge had two days of sun on it. I tried to walk laterally and stay parallel with the ridge, but I slipped and slid downhill 20 yards for every 40 yards I crossed. I stopped to gather myself and catch my breath. My heart was beating faster than it should have been for the exertion and my mind raced as it tried to calculate a solution to a problem it had not considered. I stopped and leaned on my sticks while I pondered my predicament. I couldn't afford to drop off the ridge too soon, but I kept sliding down the slope. I looked up at the ridge that grew more distant by the step; it would be no easy feat to climb back up and retrace my route to Sherman's Saddle. I looked downhill over a slope that disappeared beneath itself. It got steeper and patches of trees and rock outcroppings promised to break bones if I fell. I was in a tough situation and there was no easy way out of it.

I moved cautiously along the slope leaning up toward the ridge to compensate for the inevitable slide down and aimed for any place in between to get traction. I gained a few yards across the hill and slipped along the way. Sometimes I slid further than other times. It was unpredictable. I stopped in the trees if I got lucky; many times, I stopped only when I fell. Then I got into a shallow ravine and things got ugly in a hurry. Scrub brush hidden under the snow worked like greasy skids. I stepped on slick limbs hidden under the snow, slipped and did the splits, and fell on sharp and jagged rocks. Then I had to struggle to get back up. I took the snowshoes off, but that didn't seem to help as much as I had hoped. One thing was certain; no matter what I tried, I descended down the slope off the ridge faster than I wanted and I was still miles from Hungery Creek. I slid bug-eyed 50'- 60' before I slammed into a stand of willows. I scolded myself – to be mindful of the calamitous effect of a broken bone or dislocation.

My mind's eye created a visual of me flying through a clump of bushes, emerging to see the ground below me disappear as I began a breathtaking freefall. I was no longer just losing the ridgeline; I was losing control. Gravity was kicking my ass and I had no arresting tool; no way to stop a screaming slide. Things were way past tense.

Then I heard water in a gully. I'd always been pretty nimble when rock-hopping and had my favorite boots on. I had my Gore-Tex britches on over my boots and my dependable rubberized gaiters, so I was going to stay dry – even if the water came up to my knees. Crashing down the drainage felt like a better option than sliding off the mountain. I had given up on side-hilling Willow Ridge. I was coming down one way or another, so I looked for a safer way than chaotic cartwheels down through the rocks. The little stream and its trickling waterfalls seemed a better option than uncontrolled slides, so that's the way I went. I busted through the spindly trees that surrounded the falling water.

It was quite beautiful, actually. Especially when I remembered that the fledgling creek would inevitably merge with one or two more and they all fed the creek at the bottom which flowed to Hungery Creek. Just like Hungery Creek met with other creeks to form rivers that made life on this planet possible. And they all started with a trickle of water like the one I stepped my way down.

Unfortunately, the gully wasn't an easy climb down. It wasn't a cooperative staircase of tiny waterfalls. It made me work for my descent. It dropped ten feet as a free-falling column or blocked my passage with a thick fence of trees or teetering bone-breaking boulders. Sometimes, the only way to make progress was to grab live branches and lean on them to swing out over an obstruction. It felt so unnatural; to lean away from the waterfall and swing around it holding a handful of branches and vines. I had no choice but to trust Nature's belay. Moreover, I knew she would test me. Any lapse of concentration and Mother Nature would spank me. If I got cocky hopping rocks playing mountain man down a waterfall, Mother would loosen a rock underfoot. If I reached too far for a steadying branch, I would miss and tumble through the brush. I felt like she was angry with me for ignoring her warning signs.

Sometimes the throat of the gully was choked and I diverted downhill through the trees. And when the trees grew too thick, I angled back toward the stream again. Then the slope changed and began to level out and finally the little stream began to flow more than fall. I knew better than to be happy about it, but I made it safely down from the ridge. I wanted to breath a sigh of relief but something told me to wait.

Toward the bottom, the forest took on a different persona; the atmosphere was heavy, suffocating, and damp. It was not a place for visitors and had seen none in many years. There was an abundance of life but absolutely no trace of humanity. I couldn't even see a game trail. Just trees and plants, and moss-covered deadfall, and a thick living floor. Dead leaves and grasses and moss and ferns filled in the space between trees. Giant trees rested where they had been laid for generations. Reduced to compost, they stood testament to the quiet timelessness of that ancient place. The trees got thicker as the slope flattened out and I suddenly found myself at the foot of the ridge. Not at Hungery Creek as per the plan, but a place that the map called Doubt Creek.

"How appropriate," I sniped and shook my head in frustration.

I tried to stay cool but felt physically pissed off. The tension and anxiety of the day boiled up from inside and steamed out at Doubt Creek. I was not happy with the predicament and unsure of my decision to leave the Lolo Motorway. It was too early to give up on the Hungery Creek trail, but I wasn't where I planned to be and would not be there soon. I stopped to rest and to get my bearings. Fortunately, I was only two or three miles from my immediate target. Unfortunately, I had descended from the ridge into a wild rugged creek. One reason I ran ridges was to avoid creek bottoms.

Doubt Creek was not waiting with soft grass sidewalks. It was steep-banked, choked with rocks and vegetation, and blocked by massive fallen trees. I stood by the creek and gauged my predicament. I had escaped the ridge slide without falling to the bottom, but the scene I looked at seemed somehow worse. There was nothing but trees surrounded by deadfall, and little trees woven in between them. The living thatch closed in on me. The forest made me feel claustrophobic. It looked like all the trees that sprung from the ground since time began had gathered in that place to block my progress.

I stood in what felt like a primal forest. I couldn't climb up the hill I had just slid down and there was no easy escape from the woods. It was mid-November in the Clearwater National Forest and, if the storms came again, I'd be snowbound in a living snare – two or three miles from Hungery Creek and at least four miles from Sherman's Saddle. It would take Search & Rescue many days to get to me. My locator beacon was military grade and could mobilize SAR in hours, but cutting through miles of this thicket in the snow would take chainsaws and snowmobiles and a good bit of luck. I'd be a needle in a haystack. I had to escape on my own.

"This is why I do this," I tried to convince myself. "It's the difference between a trek and a hike. All I've got to do is stay cool."

It was true, of course. I had been pushing the edge since the early 80s. I enjoyed the study and training and the preparation that was involved. I liked the way trekking made me feel. Even in my late 50s, I felt strong and fast on the ground. I marveled at the way the human system operated under pressure. Most remarkably, stress helped me focus. I learned that preparation and training could minimize risk, but they could not eliminate The Unknown, and the unknown element of danger always kept me keen.

I looked around and quickly ascertained that trees were the biggest part of the problem. The deadfall, to be exact. Downed trees came up to my belly and were scattered like branches after a storm. In some places, trees laid across trees and great branches stabbed all around. It took time and real effort to get past each one, only to encounter another, and another. If not over or under, I could try going around but some laid over the creek. I crossed the creek and hoped for better movement only to find more of the same. The frustration factor grated on me. No matter how hard I tried to keep my cool, the steady flow of obstacles worked to wear me down. I looked up the steep mountains on both sides of the water and all I saw was trees. I tried not to think of what I should have done; better to concentrate on the challenge at hand.

I had never experienced anything as physically unnerving as the living thatch in that forest; all the lesser trees that grew by the creek - the dogwood, alder, and willow. They conspired to drive me off Willow Ridge and dumped me in Doubt Creek. Partly covered in snow, their limbs grabbed at my boots. In Doubt Creek, they grew up around the fallen trees and blocked and resisted me. I decided to cross the creek on a large moss-covered log, but the guardian trees blocked the way. Sometimes they were so thick and woven together that all I could do was lean into them. I pressed my entire weight forward and hoped they gave way. When they gave, they gave grudgingly and slapped at my head; they scratched my eyes, bruised my face, and tore my gear. More dangerously, they attacked my spirit. It was a new kind of menace to me.

The floor of the forest seemed to confirm my suspicion that no man had been there in ages. There were no sign of camps, no trails, no tracks to be found; just a carpet of ferns and rotting leaves. The patches of snow from the last storm and the permeating dampness made for slick footing in the primal forest. I fell and cursed, got lashed and cursed, climbed over trees and went on.

Still, I tried to keep my cool. I knew after I slid and tumbled off Willow Ridge that I was in harm's way. I had to keep calm and keep moving. Down there in the thicket, my route choices were few. The mountains were too steep to climb and the sides of the creek were choked by rocks and trees and shrubs. I tried literally walking in the creek, but it was deep and rocky and blocked by too much deadfall. I had to go through the forest and I had to be patient to get out.

I had to manage the two sides of me; the two sides that would keep me moving. I had to call on Pat the Optimist to stay on top of a bad situation; to believe that persistence would see me through and to keep my dark thoughts in check. I had to leverage Pat the Aggressor to press relentlessly without getting angry and out of control. I had to use my mind and my body. I had to call on both sides of me to survive the challenge ahead.

I looked at my GPS device to get my bearings. It was a little more than a couple of miles to the crossing at Hungery Creek and many more miles to my target (Hungery Camp, marked by Lewis & Clark in 1805). The sun set at 4 p.m. in the mountains in late November and I generally made camp an hour earlier. It was noon when I crossed Doubt Creek and reassessed the situation, so I had three hours to get a feel for the place before I stopped down to make camp. The canopy was so dense and the snow so thick on the tree branches I thought I might lose satellite reception. I pulled out my trusty old compass knowing that all I really had to do was head south. Failing all else, a southerly course would lead me to Hungery Creek and I could find my way out from there. My eyes adjusted to the gloom; the forest had blocked out most of the light. I searched for the path of least resistance. I could usually spot an opening through the trees, but there was no path in that mish-mash of wood. As my face drew in to a scowl of resolve, I engaged the first obstacle in my way.

After three hours of fighting the thicket, I found a spot where I could make camp. It took a healthy imagination, but there was just enough room to spread out my little tent in an opening in the undergrowth. The small opening was crisscrossed by deadfall of very large trees. Feathery prehistoric ferns grew out of the moss that filled the space where the trees came together. The forest floor was carpeted with pine needles and leaves. It was, truthfully, quite beautiful. In the midst of the grim struggle, I felt I came upon a fairy garden. It was lush and wet. But everything was wet and everything was cold.

I advanced a little more than a quarter of a mile in the span of those first three hours; a hundred something yards per hour. My base layer of clothing was soaked with sweat from crawling and thrashing and climbing. What I learned that first afternoon in the primal forest was that there would be no respite. I had encountered deadfall earlier that trip and other times while trekking, but I had never seen anything so sustained. The forest never relented. I felt it didn't want me to leave. The trapped feeling was claustrophobic; it crept into my mind and created uncertainty. I forced my mind to focus on a plan for moving forward a hundred yards at a time. The forest was a jigsaw puzzle. A Rubik's Cube. A challenge to body and mind. At the end of three hours, I sat down on a tree and ate a handful of jerky for dinner and tried to stop thinking. I needed to rest well for a full-bodied struggle the next day.

I woke in the fairy garden and dreaded the day's work ahead. I didn't want to get out of my sleeping bag; the day before had been too damned hard. It felt like too much work for a man my age; being dragged off a ridge a few thousand feet into a smothering labyrinth of towering canopies and rotting wood and leaves. It was cold and my clothes were wet. I wasn't lost but pretty damn close. I loathed looking at my barometer; the news could be very bad. Again, my mind imagined a storm and snow up to my butt cheeks. I was lucky to find refuge with a trapper the week before when the snow shut me down for two days. Then, I had a trail and could use snowshoes, and still the deep snow made it tough. If that happened in the primal forest, I... well, I couldn't afford to give room to those thoughts. I had to get up and get moving to beat out the storm and a potentially dangerous case of the blues.

I peeled off the dry polypro that I slept in and put it back in its Ziploc. I cursed under my breath as I pulled the work layer on; it was cold and wet and depressing, but worked when my body heated up. Quickly, I put on my Gore-Tex shell and started stretching to get warm. I boiled water for oatmeal and tea, and did jumping jacks to generate heat and quiet the shiver caused by my wet base layer. After I finished with my breakfast, I put my camp in my pack and turned to look south. I knew it would be difficult, but I forced myself to smile.

"Not today, no. You're not getting me today. I'll crawl through you a foot at a time, if that's what it takes to get out."

The fallen tree in front of me was probably four feet thick. There might have been a foot-and-a-half clearance beneath the tree, so I'd have to go over to gain ground. There was another deadfall just five yards past the one I faced. But there was five yards between them which was better than having to crawl over two together. The willows were present but only a few sticking up and I parted them using my poles. I threw a leg over the tree and lay down on my belly to roll across it. Sometimes I had to break off branches to make room to get by and the stubs grabbed at my clothing. More than once, they made holes in me. I often stopped to remind myself to be careful, to take it slow, and to remember that the great danger was just getting hurt. It was no exaggeration to say that a broken leg could have been a mortal wound that deep in the backcountry.

Once in a while, I saw daylight. On occasion, I took twenty or thirty steps unobstructed. I actually developed a tempo and my hopes climbed for a minute or two, then the forest took me back again.

At one place, it looked like a logging truck burst open and spilled its load on that spot. As if an earthquake had destroyed a huge Roman temple and the pillars had crashed to the ground. There was no way around it or over it or under it; I had to go to the other side of the creek. I moved to my left and wrestled with the undergrowth just to get close to the water. The foliage thinned out by the creek bank and I looked for a way to get across. I plotted a course across the rocks... a sort of hop scotch over Doubt Creek. My trekking poles helped me balance the weight of my cumbersome pack. Sometimes, that part was fun. I enjoyed bouncing across creeks. It was exciting and a little bit tricky. If nothing else, it was a distraction from my plight.

Back and forth across the creek, I searched for ways to get through. Hour by hour, I made a little progress. A hundred yards, a few dozen trees, another quarter mile behind me. Stubbornly I struggled, I worked without rest. If I could beat the next storm, I'd be fine.

After another night camped in the primal forest, after two days crawling and climbing and thrashing, at 10 o'clock in the morning, I caught sight of Hungery Creek. Cartographers left the name as it was spelled in Meriwether Lewis' journal. My excitement at finding it started when I heard it from a hundred yards away. My enthusiasm waned when it came into view. Like all the waterways in Idaho, it damn sure didn't look like a creek. It was 60 feet wide and the water was rugged. All rocks except the biggest boulders were covered by a fast moving current. I wasn't going to 'rock hop' that tumbling waterway; I'd have to ford it to get across.

I took off my boots and socks and rolled up my pants. I wanted to be happy to have arrived at Hungery Creek, but something wasn't right. I thought back on my trek through the primal forest. It had taken two days to travel about three miles. I was slow but relentlessly steady. The rip-stop fabric that made up my waterproof shell had been torn. In spite of the freezing temperatures, my base layer and socks were soaked with sweat. My titanium poles were bowed from catching my weight when thatch tried to knock me down. My left eye was rheumy where it had been slapped by a willow and the socket below it was yellow and black. I succeeded because I persisted. I got up when I was knocked down. Two days and three miles later, I should have felt elated. And I did for a couple of minutes until I caught sight of a freezing cold creek so deep and wide that it should have been called Hungery River.

I once fell through the ice on a creek in Wyoming while carrying an expedition pack. Suffice it to say that it came as a complete surprise. I still had my waist belt buckled, a requirement for heavy loads. When the ice broke beneath me, I panicked at the thought of falling in with the pack and being dragged by the current under the ice. It would take a couple of minutes to die a cold and frantic death. Every time I waded across a mountain creek or river since, I felt that electric panic flicker.

I felt it when I stepped into the big fast water of Hungery Creek, but it passed after a couple of steps. My feet felt for footing that was reliable and steady as river rocks shifted when I stepped on them. My trekking poles were out wide in opposite directions to provide the support I needed. I ignored the shocking cold and tried to find a flat place on the rock bottom and not step on something sharp or slanted. Then I put my weight on it, tenuously at first. When stability was confirmed, I moved my poles and repeated the process again. I probably wouldn't drown if I fell in, but it would be a long time before I got dry. And the Rockies in November was no place to be if you were soaking wet and freezing.

When I stepped out of the creek on the other side, I looked back at the primal forest. I thought about the struggle it presented and wished I had time to enjoy my escape, but I was too busy gearing up. I turned to face a small hill labeled Obia's Point on the map. The open sky above the creek allowed me to use my GPS device and I correlated its data with my map. Lewis & Clark crossed Hungery

Creek and went to the right for six or seven miles to camp. Hungery Camp was what they had called it and that was where I intended to go.

I faced the mountain and expected to see a trail which would take me to the right and on to Hungery Camp. Instead there were granite outcroppings on my left that jutted out into the creek and, in front of me, a 40 degree slope covered with trees and bushes. It might not sound too steep, but it was disheartening to stand face-to-face with it. It would barely hold snow but it held plenty of trees. The trail was nowhere in sight.

Obia's Cabin

It is important for the reader to remember that the reason I got trapped in the primal forest was the disappearance of the Lewis & Clark trail. It was easy to find on the north side of Willow Ridge where it angled south from Sherman's Saddle, but the trail evaporated in the snow at the crest. Even when I ran the ridge, I wondered aloud why anyone would take that route. There must have been better ways to get to the plains to the west.

"No capable pathfinder would go this way. Certainly not Meriwether Lewis," I thought.

After I struggled through a forest that was almost impenetrable, I was disappointed at the absence of a trail to Hungery Camp, but not completely surprised. I let my guard down when I emerged from the primal forest. I spent two days telling myself that things would be fine once I escaped. But they weren't fine; I had no confidence in the trail to Hungery Camp. That whole leg of the journey seemed unreliable. I remembered Trapper Joe talking about Obia's Cabin, saying it was in the direction of Fish Creek. It stood to reason that, given two separate landmarks in opposite directions, there was a trail up in front of me somewhere. Even if it didn't look like it.

I pulled on my pack and cinched it tight. Since there was no trail in front of me, I would climb up the face to find one. I walked up to the hillside and leaned into it. I leaned into the dirt and looked uphill for trees to use on my climb. The dirt was loose, so I kicked a foothold and pushed off the creek bank to go upwards. I grabbed the small trees, pulled up the slope, and kicked the toes of my boots in each step. It didn't take long to get moving. I moved 100 feet up in a hurry. A forty degree slope meant I wouldn't freefall if I fell, but I wouldn't stop tumbling either. But there were plenty of trees and my foot holds were solid; I didn't feel any anxiety. I stopped thinking and was in action mode. I would not stop until I reached the summit or the trail. I didn't have time for rest.

I steamed my way up the hill, head down and determined, and the trail appeared right before my eyes. Three hundred feet above Hungery Creek, I found a trail in the dirt. It was exhilarating! There was no fresh sign on it, but it was a real-life trail. I pulled out my GPS, let it sync, and saw I was standing on a trail on the map. The trail was, at most, a foot-and-a-half wide and it crumbled dangerously on the downhill side.

But it looked like a red carpet. I felt like the Grand Prize Winner. The trail looked like a highway after the pathfinding problems in the forest. I was elated. I had persisted and found a trail! THE trail that would take me forward with Lewis & Clark and the heroic Corps of Discovery. I put a song on my lips and made off for Hungery Camp. I was right to fight through Willow Ridge. My efforts on Doubt Creek would be rewarded. Certainly, the worst was behind me. I was back on the trail with Lewis & Clark. All the landmarks came flooding back from my memory, all the places I could choose from to make real camps. Bad times just made the good times better. And I felt things were getting better by the minute.

The trail curled around the face of the mountain and followed the contours on the map. I made observations as I moved. The trees were sparse because I was on the north side of the hill. I looked down at the map and saw that I would stay on the north side for quite a while. There wasn't much vertical gain on the hike and there were no creeks to cross. It was six miles to the Hungery Creek campsite and, if I was lucky, I would be there in two or three hours.

There were a few scattered trees in the path but nothing out of the ordinary. It was good to hike again, to take one step after another without lifting my legs to climb over a tree. Oh, occasionally there was a dead tree stretched downhill over the trail, but there were always dead trees in the forest. I stepped across the deadfall without losing stride. It felt good to stretch my legs. I loosened the pack for walking. My sticks searched for a rhythm. I looked at the sky and caught glimpses of sunlight for the first time in several days. It felt good to be moving again, good to be making progress.

Then there was another tree across the trail, then three more in a tangled pile, followed by another. I slowed down and gave it some thought; unlike the forest, the ground wasn't flat. The deadfall was not lying flat on the ground but was poised to slide down the mountain. I could go up above the trail to bypass the cluster but probably not down. It took a few minutes, but my new skills hard-won in the primal forest below were put to good use on the problem. The trail curved left around the next corner and I stopped at the turn to take in the view. After the turn, the trail went 60-70 yards and then curved to the right and I saw all the way around the crescent bend. It was like looking at the curve of a quarter-mile track and the dead trees laid across the trail like railroad ties. I thought I was hallucinating. The deadfall was like a giant picket fence that had fallen across the trail. Most were easy enough to overcome but some would take work. It was not as bad as the primal forest, but I had been through this down in the creek bottom and did not want to play on a side hill. I had been two days making three miles. How long would it take to cover the six miles to Hungery Camp? And the camps beyond that? Was this the worst of it or would the trail become progressively more difficult to travel? I felt like a boxer must feel after going ten rounds and spending a minute on his stool. And then the bell rings and he has to get up; he has to go back in the fight.

"No," I considered, "you don't have to fight. There's another option here. It's at least six miles to Hungery Camp but only a mile and a half to Obia's."

Obia's Cabin. I didn't even know if it existed. Trapper Joe had asked me to waypoint it if I found it and tell him what kind of shape it was in. But he didn't know where it was for sure and he'd been trapping in the Clearwater for decades. I didn't know if the cabin was real and if it was still intact. It might have been a story or a rustic foundation without walls. But there was a dot with its name on my map and the dot seemed to call to me.

The Lolo Trail, the Lewis & Clark path, was at least three times as far and I wasn't sure it was real, either. My barometer was steady and there was sun in the sky, but I didn't expect either to last. I planned to travel the historic trail to where the mountains tumbled into the plains. I pushed myself. I wanted to travel where they traveled and sleep where they slept.

Hungery Camp six miles to the west? Or Obia's Cabin less than two miles east? There was a pack trail near the mark for Obia's Cabin on the map and it led west; perhaps I could make it to Kooskia following it. Neither destination was totally real in my mind; both were just dots on a 2" GPS screen. I stood where I was because the trail to Hungery Camp was a clotted artery. And Hungery Camp wasn't the last stop on that journey. If I went toward the Grove, there were at least three more camps spread across a distance of 20-25 miles. That would require four long days if the trail was good and the weather stayed steady and clear. If the weather got bad and I needed to get out, it would be 10 hard miles to the highway. Obia's Cabin, however, could serve as an exit if things got bad. Because of the way the pack trail angled in, I would only be 5 miles away from safety. My ego wanted to finish what I set out to do, but logic dictated otherwise. Snow was coming sooner or later; did I want to roll the dice or play it smart?

I looked back at the trail to Hungery Camp. The deadfall looked like a fistful of chopsticks scattered on a dirty table.

"If you decide to go that way," I scolded, "after all that's happened this week… and a big storm comes… you'll deserve everything that happens to you."

I didn't argue anymore. I turned around to find Obia's Cabin.

The trail I followed towards Obia's Cabin was like the one to Hungery Camp. No matter how cluttered or difficult, it was a huge improvement over the rotting carpet in the forest. It was 12"-18" wide and eroded on the downhill side. It was three hundred feet to the water below and very steep; I would roll downhill if I slipped or if the trail gave way until I hit something or tumbled into the creek. It was very serious, treacherous at times, and counterproductive to think about it much. But at least there was a trail, for a time.

Then there were the big shrubs and small trees that had grown out of the hill and deadfall that blocked my way. Not nearly as much as to the west, but there was always deadfall. My long legs let me straddle some trees and others I crawled under. Sometimes I grabbed living shrubs or tree branches. Branches in hand, I leaned out over the steep slope and trusted the branches to hold as anchors so I could swing around obstacles on the hill. It wasn't as bad as the last several days, but almost; the risk was actually higher from time to time. I learned from the forest and was savvy; I had technique that I had learned along Doubt Creek. I felt I could make it that day if I pushed it. It wasn't too far according to the map. The open runs were longer and I was able to stay on the trail. It disappeared sometimes but I knew where to go. And my adrenaline was pumping; I did not feel tired. There was a sense of urgency that drove me.

Unfortunately, I lost the trail only a quarter mile from Obia's Cabin. I tried not to panic, but I felt at my wits' end. I looked all over, but the small creeks feeding Hungery Creek spread out and created hidden bogs. The mud bogs camouflaged the trail. I stepped into one that felt like muddy quicksand. It sucked my foot in up to my knee and I had a hard time getting out. It took a focused effort to keep moving forward.

"So I crossed the Hungery River and climbed up the side of a mountain on my goddam hands and knees. I find the trail and it's blocked? Now there's quicksand sucking my boots off?"

I felt frustration growing and had to work hard to keep my cool.

I descended to the level of the creek in my search for the cabin and worked back and forth from the water's edge to the high side of the bottom. I kept moving around the dot on my map. My GPS device said I had arrived, but the cabin was nowhere to be found. I walked back and forth past the dot on the map used by the GPS. My tracks looked like I had one leg tied down; I was going around in circles. I was sorely disappointed: a three-day ass-beating, a scratched cornea from whipping branches, a cut under an eye from a limb strike, torn and bruised elbows, bumps and bruises and humiliation from several dozen falls, and nothing to show for it. No reward. Just mud on my boots and a bruised attitude. Worse, it was 2:45 p.m. and I had to find a camp site and find one right away. So I swallowed my frustration and moved away from the dot and on to find a place to camp.

I moved forward less than 100 yards and, out of the corner of my eye, I spotted a meadow on the other side of the creek. It provided a measure of relief; a port in a storm. A meadow would provide some soft flat ground on which to stretch out and rest. There might even be room to build a fire. But the meadow was on the other side of Hungery Creek. If I had to ford that damn creek again to get a good night's sleep, so be it. Just one more problem in a day full of them.

"A meadow would be a welcome change of pace," I admitted and consoled myself with the compromise as I veered toward the creek's bank. I walked downstream and looked for a place to cross.

And suddenly, it appeared; a ramshackle trapper's cabin in the middle of the meadow. It was on the opposite side of the creek than it was mapped, but it had to be Obia's place. With what I'd been through those last three days, it looked like the Taj Mahal!

I was so relieved, so glad to have chosen that path. So happy with my decision to play it safe. I let go of the need to follow the Lewis & Clark trail and was only a few yards from my reward for making the right decision. I made my bones as a mountain man and knew I would rest well on that fortuitous night.

The cabin was built as a one-room shack. The siding still had some brown in it, but the shake roof had aged to gray long ago. There were two open windows on opposite sides and a door propped against one of the outside walls. The old wood stove tilted where the floor caved in, but the metal bunk bed frame looked intact. I laid in my sleeping bag on my air mattress on the bed spring and smiled as I looked out the hole where the door used to be. I watched Hungery Creek as it rolled by. It no longer seemed hostile and cold; it relaxed me with a comforting sound. I saw out cracks in the roof. A chilly breeze blew through the cabin. I laid my gear out, enjoyed a small feast, and recovered from difficult days.

I made a waypoint of its location for Trapper Joe since it was incorrectly marked on the maps. I took a lot of pictures so Joe could see what kind of shape it was in. The next day, I built a good-sized fire to dry out everything in my pack. I also took a reconnaissance hike and learned that an old pack trail passed through the camp in the meadow. My map showed that taking the pack trail west led to some logging roads that could get me to Lolo Creek, the planned terminus of my trek. It wasn't exactly the planned route but, as I had been warned, parts of the Lewis & Clark trail sorely lacked maintenance and had all but disappeared. In the other direction (southeast), the pack trail led to Fish Creek and the Clearwater trailhead where outfitters entered the forest. I was safe and warm at Obia's place, but the bottom-line question remained the same... the difference being that the pack trail was better maintained than the Lewis & Clark trail. Should I take the pack trail 25 miles to end of the Rockies? Or walk along Fish Creek to the Wilderness Gateway?

When I got back to the cabin, I was dismayed to see I burned holes in the two pair of socks I had brought. One was so badly burned, I had to repair it with duct tape. Not a patch, mind you; I put the burned sock on my foot, brought the two burned ends together, then wound duct tape around my foot until the new tube sock was complete.

I enjoyed a dinner of tuna, dehydrated soup, and a soul-soothing cup of tea. I did a quick inventory of my remaining food. I had five tuna pouches, two servings of oatmeal, and three servings of soup. Stretched out, it was minimum rations for five days max. In good weather, I could cover the 25 miles I needed to complete the hike. Theoretically. My desire to finish the trek as planned was tempered by the knowledge that storms had pinned me down once. Had they come hard while I was bushwhacking in Doubt Creek, I'd have Been in serious trouble. I decided to wait until morning to decide, and fell asleep listening to Hungery Creek.

I slept in Obia's Cabin on the springs of the bottom bunk. I woke up at 7 a.m., looked out the open doorway, and saw eight inches of fresh snow blanketing the scene. It still fell from a sleepy sky and my barometer was flat-lined at the bottom. That meant a big low-pressure cell settled in and wasn't going anywhere soon. I smiled because the decision had been made for me. There was no way I was going all the way west with meager supplies in a storm. I spent two nights at Obia's Cabin and my adventure following Lewis & Clark was about to come to an end.

I took my time packing up, then took off on the southeast route. It was great to be on a good trail again. Even with the snowfall, the trail was easy to track. I followed the pack trail along Fish Creek until I reached the trailhead by Wilderness Gateway. I didn't rush it, even though the adventure was as good as over. It was only five miles to the road and five miles on a good trail didn't seem very far to me. With every step down the trail, with every snowflake on my skin, I knew the trek had reached its end. I wanted to savor every sight, sound, and smell. There are always other adventures but never quite like the one you're on at the time. It was a few miles before I fully realized I was done with the Lolo Trail.

When I got to the highway by the Clearwater trailhead, I was more than forty miles from Lochsa Lodge. A three-day hike. I hoped to find a ride with rangers, but the ranger station was closed. I either had to hike to Lochsa Lodge or hitchhike up the highway. I hoped to get a ride before dark. Unfortunately, not a lot of cars traveled that road in November; four or five came along, slowed down as they looked at me, and drove on up the dark road. I was frustrated at first, but I couldn't blame them. I was tall, filthy, and had a long knife at my side. I had wrestled with the forest for several long weeks and lost badly for the last five days. I don't know why I thought someone would give me a ride.

I came across a huge well-equipped rest area on the side of Highway 12 not far from the closed ranger station. I called the Highway Department from an Emergency Phone near the restrooms.

"Hello. Idaho Highways."

"Hi. This isn't a real emergency. I know it's an emergency phone, but I have to be honest and tell you that this isn't life-or-death. It's not that kind of emergency, but it is an emergency to me."

"Thank you, sir. How would you like me to help you today?"

I tried to imagine her desk, her place of work. Were there co-workers around? Was I on a speaker phone?

"Well, I'm stuck on Highway 12 in the middle of nowhere and I need a ride. I would like you to call a police officer, a highway department employee, one of the guys that drives a snow plow… anybody, and ask them to pick me up. I am at the rest stop across from Wilderness Gateway and the place looks completely shut down. I need a ride to Lochsa Lodge and there's nobody here."

"That facility is closed for the season, sir. The Forest Service has closed many of its facilities."

"Yes, ma'am. I'm sorry, but it's like this. I just came out of seven weeks in the mountains. I planned to find transport at a ranger station that I just learned is closed. That leaves me 40 miles from my destination, ma'am. 40 miles from Lochsa Lodge. I need to find a ride up Highway 12 from Wilderness Gateway to Lochsa Lodge. It would take days to walk there from here. I need help, right?"

"I'm sorry, sir, but we do not have the resources…"

"Oh, yes, ma'am. I understand that anything you do to help me will be coming straight out of your generous heart. And I can tell you sincerely that anything you can do will go a long way tonight. I don't want to roll this sleeping bag out on the side of Highway 12. A dump truck. I'll ride in the back of a dump truck. A snowplow. Is Mitch around? Doesn't he drive a snowplow?"

"Please stand by."

Then she said she would call me back, which made me wonder what she was doing and who might be watching or listening to her do it. It could be that half the road crew listened to me beg for a ride to the lodge and she wanted to give them time to laugh. It probably wasn't the kind of call they got very often, but I didn't care. I wanted a hot shower. I wanted hot food. I wanted a 45-minute ride instead of a walk that would take an extra three days. I stood huddled over a sheet metal phone in a desolate parking lot in a desolate place. I waited because she might find help. I waited because I had nothing better to do. I kept waiting and finally the phone rang.

"Hello?"

"Hello, this is the Highway Department."

"Yes, ma'am. This is me. This is the guy who called."

"Yes, sir. I'm sorry, sir, but no one seems to be in your area. Highway 12 doesn't see a lot of traffic this time of year. I contacted a couple of troopers even. I did have one tow truck driver that said he'd be coming up that road in a couple of hours or so."

"A couple hours? You're joking with me, right?"

"No, sir. I'm sorry. You might call some tow trucks or maybe a taxi in Missoula."

"Call someone in Missoula? I don't know anyone in Missoula!"

"I'm sorry, sir. We just don't have the resources."

"What if I said this WAS an emergency?"

"I'm sorry, sir."

"Okay, never mind. Thank you. Thank you for trying. I appreciate it."

Call a taxi in Missoula, is that what she suggested? On what, my Locator Beacon? Or maybe the sheet metal emergency phone? In a flash of insight, I understood why the phone was made of metal.

I had a couple more cars drive by and slow down, but no one gave serious thought to picking up the mangy gray bigfoot in orange. No one until Bob Russell came along. Perhaps his eyesight was failing or he just was in the habit of making bad decisions. There was no good explanation for it, but Bob Russell stopped to give me a lift.

He opened the rear glass in his compact SUV to make room for my pack and loose gear. He looked comfortably presentable and his breath smelled like conference room coffee. He was friendly and made me feel welcome. He was happy to take me to Lochsa Lodge and I knew I would get there in time for dinner. As it turned out, Bob was a retired Forest Service hand. In all his years as a Ranger and Forest Supervisor, he had never heard of anyone attempting, much less succeeding, a crossing of the Lolo Trail in November. He was curious and complimented me on my findings. The great irony was that Bob was on his way home from a meeting in Orofino, Idaho; a meeting of the state-wide Lewis & Clark Historical Preservation committee. We talked about trail maintenance and the importance of keeping the Lewis & Clark legacy alive.

"It's a national landmark, Bob," I declared. "The trail has significant historical value. You'd think they'd have money for maintenance. They build half-million dollar potties by the side of the road, but the Lewis & Clark trail can't be maintained?"

As he dropped me off at Lochsa Lodge, we agreed to meet in Salmon and talk about working together. In the long run, nothing came of it.

The committee was made up mostly of great thinkers and poor doers. Bob was not like them but knew them to be so, and our meeting in Salmon was more about coffee than furthering a cause.

After Bob dropped me off, I was met at the lodge by Mike. He was most excited to see me.

"I can't believe it!" he said as he momentarily forgot about his customers in the convenience store. He slapped me on the back and celebrated as though I was the first man to reach the North Pole. Mike was a retired Ranger, Search and Rescue hand, and all-round mountain man. We met when I passed through. He had worked in the Clearwater area of Idaho for decades and was fascinated with my journey.

"Hello, Mike. Didya' miss me, man?" I grinned through my grimy whiskers.

"Sorry, folks," Mike said to the couple waiting for his service. "This is Pat Taylor. He just finished walking across the Rockies. Alone."

The young man stepped forward and shook my hand. I admired his jacket.

"Arc'Teryx, man. Great gear." I nodded, gave him a thumbs up, and pointed to the logo on my shell. He looked at me strangely, as if I had teeth missing or great boogies dangling from my nose.

"I mean he just finished," Mike struggled to clarify for the young couple standing in his store. "He literally just came off the trail. Been gone, what, two months?"

"Seven weeks," I corrected. "Maybe a little less."

"No shit?" the young man came to life. "You've been bouncing down Lolo in November? I rode that in the summer once and it was a bitch then!"

"Pat, this is Sam. He's an Olympic mountain bike racer. Sam and Angie, this is Pat. He's a trekker from the Lone Star State."

I didn't know they had mountain biking in the Olympics.

"Yeah, it got ugly in a spot or two."

"Where?" quizzed Mike.

"Willow Ridge. The trail just disappears."

"Course it does. Maps show it petering out right at the crest. Almost like Lewis got to the top, said 'This don't look right', and went another way."

"That's exactly what it looked like. But I found Obia's Cabin, Mike. Trapper Joe asked me to mark it if I found it. It was a sight for sore eyes, I'll tell you that."

"You met Trapper Joe. What a coincidence."

"Sure did. Up by his camp. I spent a couple days with him during the storm. He said he'd drop my pistol off here."

Mike shook his head as he looked behind the counter for Big Thump.

"Ol' Joe's a living legend. I talk with him at the store here, but no one really knows him here. Real quiet guy. Amazing for you two to run into each other on the Lolo Trail."

The young couple were waiting to finish their transaction.

"Are you going to eat dinner later?" Sam asked. "We'd like to buy you dinner if you care to share more of your story. You up for that?"

"I'll need a shower first. Think I'll get a cabin. Meet me in the restaurant in 45 minutes or an hour?"

"See you there. Take your time."

A hot shower, clean clothes, and a hot meal while trading tales about the backcountry. I loved the adventurous life!

The Next Adventure

My cousin picked me up at Lochsa Lodge, but we stayed a few days to relax and to express my appreciation for her support before heading back to civilization. Brenda was pivotal to the success of the trek and, ironically, in the adventure that was to follow.

Brenda worked as a bookkeeper for several small businesses in Salmon, one of which was a mechanic's shop. After retrieving me, she retold the tale of my trek with great enthusiasm to the owner of the garage. Sitting in the waiting room was a customer; a short wiry man with sharp features and a bushy mustache. He occasionally looked up from the magazine that he read and listened more closely to Brenda's tale. Finally, he asked her if the man she spoke of was still in town.

"He's my cousin and he's staying at my home right now."

"Would you have him call me, please?" asked the customer and handed Brenda his business card.

She called me ten minutes later. I called the man immediately and we met for lunch that day.

The man's name was Ron Ens. He owned and operated Middle Fork Outfitters and he needed a winter caretaker. I was doing nothing at the time and he liked that I was comfortable being alone in the backcountry. His ranch sat on the edge of one of the largest wilderness areas in the Lower 48.

"That's your cousin works at the garage?"

"Yes, sir."

"She says you spent October in the Selway and run the Lolo just last month. That true?"

"Yes, sir. I started Lolo at Wendover Ridge."

"Gets nasty up there. You go it alone?"

"Yes, sir."

"I need a man that can live alone in the backcountry for a month or more at a time. You that man?"

"I got no problem being alone."

"You know stock?"

"Sir?"

"Stock. Horses and mules. Do you know anything about stock?"

"No, sir."

"You call yourself a mountain man and don't know anything about stock? A mountain man had to have stock to carry his traps and pelts and other truck. Can't be a mountain man if you don't know stock."

He baited me and smiled as he leaned over his lunch. I laughed out loud.

"What's so funny?"

"I spent the last two months alone in the Clearwater and Selway. I can live alone in the trees and stones without human contact for months at a time. And have a good time doing it. Ain't that a mountain man?"

Ron's grin lifted the ends of his generous mustache.

"I guess you'll do," he nodded. "I need you at the ranch on the 14th. Call me if something comes up."

Two weeks later, I was on the road. It was about 40 miles from Highway 93 back to the B - C Ranch (the "B Bar C"; Ron's place). I was to meet Ron at the ranch on December 14th. I loaded my pack and left Salmon on the 10th. I caught a ride to the Forest Service road that eventually led to the ranch. Compared to the trek I made in October and November, the trip to Ron's would be no more than a long hike.

I made nine miles with a forty pound pack in the course of that first afternoon. I found a nice wide spot and set up camp in the snow by the side of the road. I lay down to sleep a couple hours after dark. I woke up chilly at about 1 a.m., which was a bit of a surprise because my sleeping bag was rated for 20 below. I put on a jacket and went back to sleep.

In that drowsy hour before I finally got up, I heard several vehicles pass by my site. I was a little surprised since it was so late in the year. But there were ranchers and outfitters that used that road to get to their stock or get wood. When I got up and started breaking camp, a pickup stopped and the window rolled down.

"Hey, man. You alright?" asked the driver.

"Living like a king," I replied and extended a hand. "My name is Pat Taylor."

"Hello, Pat Taylor. I'm Clay Jones," he said. "If you don't mind me askin'," he asked as his grin grew wider, "what the hell you doin' out here?"

"Just hired on with Ron Ens for a while. Told him I'd be there by Saturday, so I'm enjoying this weather and working my way back."

"You goin' to work for Ron? Hell, that's another 30 miles from here! Throw your gear in the back; I'll give you a ride."

"No thanks, Clay. I can make 30 miles by Saturday easy. It's bad style to show up at a man's house unannounced."

Clay stared at me out of the open window of his truck. His face was frozen in thought. There was too much non-compliant data to process: 'No, I'd rather walk 30 miles', 'Showin' up early's bad style?' What does that even MEAN? Camping in zero-damn-degrees...

"Goddam, man; its -11 this morning; 11 degrees below zero. That's too damn cold, ol' hand."

"When I start pissin' popsicles is when it's too damn cold, my friend. And if it gets like that, I'll just crawl back in my bag a while," I grinned.

Clay's spontaneous laugh-spasm sprayed tobacco juice over the lower half of his windshield.

""Pissin' popsicles!" he coughed. "What the fuck? Where you from, Pat Taylor"

"Texas," I said all puffed up with pride.

"Sonofabitch," he said and turned to his passenger. "Did you hear that? From Texas and he's sleepin' outside in Idaho... right in the middle of December." Turning back to me, he answered, "You goddam Texans are either crazy as hell or tougher'n boiled owl."

He still sputtered and coughed from the Copenhagen he'd swallowed.

"Now, Clay, I need you to promise that you won't mention this to Ron. I like the time I get to myself and he isn't expecting me for days."

"I won't tell him, but I can't promise I won't answer a question. Ain't but a thousand people in Challis and 8 or 10 have probably seen you already. Gonna be a lot of people wonderin' who the hell is sleepin' in a tent up Morgan Creek right now. That Tuggle the Postman will say somethin' for sure. If Ron knows you're a backcountry hand, he'll probably figure it out. If he asks me, I got to answer, but I won't offer anything up. I can promise you that."

"Fair enough, Clay. Thanks for stopping."

"Had to make sure you were alive, ol' dude. You need me to bring anything when I roll back by?"

"Water would be nice... just a bottle or two. I can't chip through that frozen creek and I burn too much fuel melting snow."

"Water it is and maybe a beer," he said with a wink and he was off to cut a truck full of wood.

I had four or five hours on my boots that day when a long truck and horse trailer slowed to a crawl coming towards me. I recognized the driver; it was my new boss. He rolled down the window and nodded his head.

"Hello, Ron." I said.

"Hello, Pat," he smiled. "Decided on walkin' out? Not surprised. Best way to see the country. I'm goin' to town to drop off a horse. Pick you up on my way back?"

"I don't mean to interfere. You weren't expecting me 'til Saturday," I said.

"Extra time together means you're better prepared for the job. Enjoy the country while you can; you prob'ly won't get far from the ranch once I leave. Want me to take your pack?"

I grinned my favorite Cheshire grin, shook my head, and shrugged.

"I reckon not," he smiled. "How far will you be up the road?"

"8 miles, maybe more."

"You got to make it past that summit if you gonna make 8 miles."

"I've made a summit before, Ron," I winked. "If you aren't back an hour before dark, I'm going to set up camp and catch you tomorrow."

I walked north and he drove south.

It was a whole new incarnation of me walking in the backcountry. There were qualities in me that never would have come out had I not risked the trek. I was at peace again; the peace coming as a byproduct of acceptance. It came from being happy with my life... happy with living for adventure. I knew it was my new work in this life and was happy to have realized it.

I drifted up toward the summit of the hill where Panther Creek and Morgan Creek run off in different directions. As I neared the switchbacks that carved the way to the top of the mountain in the shadows, I smiled at the change in temperature and light. For those who choose to enter the dark folds on a mountain's face, it gets darker and colder as you near the summit. I lengthened and strengthened my stride and lifted my chest against the load. Powering through the last couple miles to a summit makes it that much sweeter coming off the top.

About a quarter mile before I cleared the pass, Ron pulled up with pizza and deliciously cold beer. I tossed my pack in the back of his truck. We got reacquainted while we sat on the trailer and ate and shared the mountain sunset. I was happy to start a new adventure in the wilderness. I was going to learn so much.

T🏔AS YETI BOOKS

Dear Reader,

Thanks for sharing this adventure with me!

Now that you've finished "Lost on Purpose", perhaps you can spare a minute to share your feedback. Honest reviews help readers find the right book for their tastes and reading needs. If you feel so inclined, please return to the "Lost on Purpose" book page on Amazon, scroll down to 'Write a Review', and share your valued opinion.

Thanks for participating,

Pat

Your Free Book is Waiting!

Long before I decided to get "Lost on Purpose",
I began to live an intentionally adventurous life.
This full-length prequel (rated 4+/5 stars by Amazon readers)
is the perfect introduction to the
'Real-life Adventures of the Texas Yeti'.
And it's free!